Testimonials

"We did all of the different surveys, the DISC survey, and all of these other different surveys…we invested so much time (and money) on all of these different assessments (and conference, etc.)…After I (took) all of the twelve, thirteen, fifteen (different) assessments, and learned about how I work with teams and all of these different things…I have to say, I was at the end of it! None of it was coming together for me…I said, 'How do we put all of this together for our people? We need to be able to apply this somehow. Put it together, so we can really help them understand, who they are, what they need, where they are going.'

When I got your profile…my mouth was hanging open when I read the graph and where I fit because it was so on target.

I was just astounded. And I wanted to tell. I am just so blessed by this.

It's really just helping people find out who they are in the Father, in His Heart first. And I think that this is just such an awesome foundation for that, because it really helps people recognize their gifts, their abilities, their talents, their motivations, just all of the different aspects of…there are so many different assessments things out there, this is just kind of like a big funnel and it brings it together. I think it is wonderful."
Pamela Oehlberg

"I know I'm the one who answered the questions, but your description of the Educator was so accurate that I could have written it about myself."
Jeff Gossett, Chief Executive Officer
Tailwinds Consulting

"The Passport revealed that I wasn't pursuing the dreams and desires of my heart. It was like this test put a mirror up to me and said, 'this is clearly what you should be doing, so why aren't you?' After that…I began pursuing what I was always meant to pursue! I am thriving…now…because it helped me to realize what I always knew and confirmed what I had always wanted. I would highly recommend this tool and resource to anyone who feels confused about

their direction in life. This test is a gateway to helping you explore that anything is possible for your life. Seeing it on paper…was the wake up call that I needed to stop being afraid of the unknown and my journey, and begin to embrace the exciting possibilities in front of me. The Passport test really did change the course of my life. I am very thankful."
Marie Joy Hunt, Executive Director
Creativity Coming Alive

"Having grown up in church, I was taught the traditional five-fold ministry concept. However, I always had a sense for entrepreneurship but did not quite know how to fit it all together. I had always been told that I was called to be an evangelist, but within the church. After completing the assessments of the *Passport to Your Identity*™, I could not believe the results! Again, I came out as a Proclaimer but this time it was not within the context of the church. I came out as a Proclaimer in the Business Mountain and the Arts and Entertainment Mountain. I was very certain that no matter what, I will always be in the Business Mountain but I was quite surprised how it picked up the Arts and Entertainment Mountain. But a light went on after learning how the Proclaimer looks within the Business Mountain, as well as in combination with the Arts and Entertainment Mountain.

As much as I love creating things and coming up with new business ideas, I love marketing and sales even more. I can tell people about products or services that I like, all day long, and gather them around certain causes that I believe in. No wonder that it was always me who organized all the parties! After doing the *Passport to Your Identity*™, I finally could accept that I am 100% Proclaimer but within the business mountain, functioning as a marketing and sales manager who loves to sell products in a creative and entertaining way."
Paul Knapp, President and CEO
KNAPP USA, Inc.

"Utilizing the *Passport to Your Identity*™ with a small group of ladies was thought provoking. The results of their assessments brought to light dreams and passions that many had laid down. Through discussion about those dormant dreams, a new realization about possibilities arose. An understanding that it was "not too late" for them to walk in their God given purpose and design began to bubble up in their spirits as they looked to

discover what steps they needed to begin walking it out."
Jody Monkus, Director of Women's Ministry
Next Level Church

"The *Passport to Your Identity*™ training has really given me great insight into how I have been designed as a person. I have taken many spiritual gifts tests, personality tests, and have a Sociology degree, but I can honestly say that the combination of the approaches in this training give a much better comprehensive view of me as a whole person. I took this class at a time when I questioned if I was qualified to lead the ministry I founded, and shortly before I became a first-time mom to 2 sons we hope to adopt. As I read through my results, it was confirmed through exact wording of the mission of my ministry in one of my strengths, that I was indeed where I needed to be to flourish as a leader. It also confirmed to me that I am a Nurturer. And I needed to know that in a concrete way as I became an overnight mom and questioned my ability to mother well. I would highly recommend this course. You will be surprised and encouraged to see your place in this world and how your gifts can be maximized to make a real difference."
Erin Blackmore, Executive Director
HopeMatch

"For more than thirty years, I have searched for my specific calling in the Kingdom of God. I tried all sorts of jobs in the church. They were all OK, but I wasn't sold. I told my husband when we met, 'I am not the typical pastor's wife who plays the piano and sings'. Having taken other spiritual gifts tests in the past, I was skeptical about *Passport to Your Identity*™. The first week into it, I was still unsure. I am so glad I stuck it out because I have finally found my niche—as a business and marketing manager for my husband's ministry! Words cannot express how grateful I am to *Passport to Your Identity*™ for allowing me to discover my identity (and purpose) in the Kingdom of God."
Faith Oliver
CPC Medical Coder

"*Passport to Your Identity*™ is not a spiritual gifts test, personality profile, character analysis, vocational quiz, career assessment, or communication style survey. It is all of these and much, much more, because *Passport to Your Identity*™ combines the results of all of these inventories into one incredibly scientific and astoundingly accurate profile.

It all begins with the Word of God and a revolutionary concept surrounding Ephesians chapter four. A careful study of Ephesians 4 reveals that all Christian believers are to live a life worthy of their calling and vocation, and that each has been given at least one special gift by God that we are to fulfill both in the church and in the world. After Christ died, rose from the dead, and ascended to heaven as triumphal king, he distributed special gifts among his people. This is a difficult truth to grasp—especially for those of us who have heard all our lives that these gifts were reserved exclusively for clergy. But at the time Paul wrote this, the organized church did not exist. If you will let it, this assessment can and will revolutionize your life, as I know it has mine. There is nothing more affirming than to know you are in God's perfect will fulfilling His call on your life. I believe *Passport to Your Identity*™ will be mightily used by God to bring unity, maturity, and growth to the whole body of Christ."
Jeff Oliver
Founder and president
Global Wakening

Dedication

I dedicate this book first and foremost to the Most High God, my Savior Jesus and Holy Spirit. This work is truly an "inspire"-ation. Without your Spirit, the revelations in this book would not have been exposed. I only pray, that I have done the glory and magnificence of Your design and plan for bringing The Kingdom to Earth justice, through what I have brought to paper.

Secondly, I dedicate this book to my mother Gertrud whose great faith in God and her commitment to The Lord gave me the model and the foundation for my own faith. I also dedicate this book to my father Klaus, who modeled a stick-to-it and don't-give-up kind of lifestyle. It was the standard of his tenacity that helped me to complete the course set before me, finish the task, and produce the work that you are holding in your hands. I am looking forward to seeing you both again in Heaven.

Finally, I dedicate this book to all of my fellow English teachers and those who are pedantic with respect to the English language and its usage. Many will scour this book for mistakes and note issues in the usage and placement of periods in proximity to quotation marks. This book was written while I resided in Europe and it reflects the more relaxed British English usage of the punctuation.

Table of Contents

Table of Illustrations

Table of Tables

Foreword by Ivan Tuttle

Proclaimer and Internationally Best–Selling Author of *A Journey to Hell, Heaven, and Back*

When I was asked to write the foreword to Sylvia Nitz's new book, I was honored to be the one to tell the world about her.

Sylvia is one of the most dedicated people I have ever known, when it comes to things about the Lord. I personally know that she not only does research, but she spends much time in prayer talking to God about what she is to write about. When she writes about a subject, you know that she not only believes it, she lives it!

Having read her new book, I will tell you that my eyes were opened to things that I had never thought of before. She gets so in-depth on a subject and finds a way to take you there with her. When you finish reading her new book, actually, any book she writes, you will walk away with more knowledge than you may initially realize. I know that Sylvia is guided by the leading of the Holy Spirit, not only in her writings, but also in her personal walk with the Lord.

Your eyes will be opened to so much more than has been revealed before, when she takes you back through the history of the Seven Mountain Mandate. You will learn when this movement actually started and I promise you, it will be a surprise!

There is one section in the book that meant more to me than I could ever write about. Sylvia had me go through an assessment to find out exactly where my strong points are within the Seven Mountains. But, it goes much deeper than that; the assessment helped me and will help you to find exactly what your position is within that section of the mountain and what other parts of the mountain you belong in. As you read the book, you too will start seeing your direction more clearly.

I have known Sylvia for some time now. We have had many discussions about different topics on the Lord, the Holy Spirit and the Bible. Each time, I have walked away from those conversations feeling like I have gained knowledge. It would be so easy for me to write about everything I have read about in this eye-opening book. But then, I think you need to read it yourself and find all those things in it that fit you.

I, myself, am a Proclaimer. After you read this book, you will have a deeper knowledge and understanding as to what that means. I know I did. This is why I feel I am blessed to have met and to know her!

I challenge you to read this book and ask the Holy Spirit to open your eyes and your heart to hear what God has given her to write to the Body of Christ about. It really is a roadmap to help "Your Kingdom Come on Earth!"

Preface

I had been an architect, a city planner, a teacher of English as a second language to adult business people, a moderator of an internationally broadcast radio show, an adjunct professor at the local university, and a PhD student doing research and finalizing text for my doctoral thesis before that fateful day in Riga, Latvia. I had also been a Christian with a deep and longstanding relationship with, a faith in, and a holy love (and fear) of God. That love/fear of God and obedience to Him led me to hop on a plane and travel across Europe to attend a conference at a small, independent Russian church on the outskirts of downtown Riga. I had no idea at the time, but my life would never be the same again.

It was my second trip to Latvia and my second trip to that particular church. I had just finished writing my first book, which was based upon research that I had been doing about quality of life in cities. As I took my usual place at the back of the church, The Lord spoke to me. "Sylvia." "Yes, Lord." "Do you see the prophet at the front of the room?" "Yes, Lord." "The one who prophesied over you the last time that you visited this church?" "Yes, Lord." "The one who told you that your life had been very difficult, but that it would be getting better?" "Yes, Lord." "Is your life better now, Sylvia?" "Yes, Lord." "Don't you think he would like to hear about that and would be encouraged to hear how much his obedience to me has helped you?"

I knew it was a set-up. The first time I had visited Latvia, that prophet had "read my mail". He told me things about my life, about my pain, about hopes and disappointments that I had never shared with anyone except God before. He told me about myself. He **really** read my mail. I think I cried harder during the time that he was ministering to me, than I think I have ever cried in my entire life. They were wracking sobs. They were deep, into-your-very-soul kind of sobs.

So, honestly, to confess, I had seen the Russian prophet and I had been avoiding him. I had had the sneaking suspicion that if I met him or spoke with him, The Lord would use him to shake me to the core again. And I had absolutely no intention of allowing that to happen. So I had been avoiding him. And The Lord knew. And He called me on it. God really knows you. He knows all of your hopes and fears. He knows you so well, that He can use your character traits and core beliefs to motivate you to do things that you may not even want to do. That's what He did with me. God used the one thing He knew my innermost convictions and beliefs would not allow me to reject. He used manners.

I grew up in a home with two immigrant parents. My parents were both German and my mother was born into a very old German family. Actually, one side of my mother's family is an old German family of nobility. So manners were important. Then, through a set of life circumstances, I ended up living in Europe for a long time. Europeans believe in manners. All of this led to a core belief of mine that manners are extremely important. I believe that they serve to regulate relationships between individuals. Manners are the rules, by which the game of life is played. And God knew that.

God used my core belief in the value of manners and my inner conviction that manners are vitally important in life, to compel me to say thank you to that prophet. I couldn't have said no to God, even if I had wanted to. He had logically argued me into a corner. Refusing to go and say thank you to someone who had helped me would have violated a core belief of mine. He had me.

So I took a deep breath and walked to the front of the church. I had the proof version of my first book with me, which I wanted to show him. My intention was to show him the book, to thank him for his previous ministrations, and then to beat a hasty retreat to the back of the church as fast as possible. God had other plans and I suspected that.

My suspicions were correct.

When I reached the Russian prophet, I re-introduced myself. He recognized me. Then I thanked him, reached into my bag, and pulled out the proof copy of my book to show him. I was holding on to his hand and holding out the book to him. He took it. Then I felt an angel grab my left wrist and begin to tug on it. I had been had, and I knew it. Being German, I had that traditional characteristic of most German people. Some call it persistence; others call it tenacity; still others call it stubbornness. I was stubborn. And I freely admitted it. I knew it was a set-up, I knew that the strength of the angel's tugging meant that God had some serious plans for me. But I was not going to go down without a fight.

So I held on tighter. The angel was increasing the force of the tugging on my wrist, and I was holding on to that Russian prophet for dear life. It was a tug-of-war between that angel, the Russian prophet and myself. That Russian prophet had absolutely no clue what was happening, except that a stubborn German, who was not going into her fate without a serious fight, was slowly crushing his arm. Angels are strong. Actually, angels are **REALLY** strong. What I realized, after I couldn't hold on to the prophet's arm any longer and finally let go, was that there were two angels in that altercation. As soon as I let go of the Russian prophet's arm, the other angel grabbed my other wrist. The first angel spun me around, both angels lifted me off the ground and then they slammed me to the ground. I hit the ground so hard, that an earring popped off of my ear and flew through the air. The angels must have been angry because I fought with them. I am convinced of this, because of the force with which they spun me, lifted me and then slammed me to the ground. It was not pretty. It certainly was not gentle.

They pinned me to the ground, with both arms extended to the side, in the same manner that Jesus had been pinned to the Cross. Then the Spirit of God began to be imparted into my spirit. Honestly, I think I pissed off a number of heavenly beings that day, because that impartation could not, in any way, shape or form, have been considered tender. In fact, it felt like I was being punched in the stomach—over and over and over again.

By now, the Russian prophet was kneeling by my head, and an interpreter was kneeling beside him. As I was being punched in the stomach…sorry…as the Spirit of God was being imparted into my Spirit Man (for those of you who prefer "Christianese"), the Russian prophet began to share the words of The Father to me. The Lord began to speak through scripture.

"The Spirit of the Sovereign Lord is upon you…" The first response that popped into my head was a very dry, "No kidding." The prophet continued reciting the words of God, "because The Lord has anointed you to proclaim good news to the poor, He has sent you to bind up the brokenhearted, and to proclaim freedom for the captives and release from darkness for the prisoners." I recognized the source of this scriptural text. It came from Isaiah

61 and it was the text that Jesus read in the temple during His first public sermon. I was struggling to try to pay attention to the words that the prophet was speaking, because I was being punched in the stomach at the same time.

So, to me, the event played out like this. "The Spirit of the Sovereign Lord is upon you." OOF. "Because The Lord has anointed you…" OOF. "To proclaim good news to the poor…" OOF. "He has sent you to bind up the brokenhearted…" OOF. "…and to proclaim freedom for the captives…" OOF. "…and the release from darkness…" OOF. "…for the prisoners." OOF. Then the Russian prophet kept repeating the same phrase over and over. "Set the captives free, set the captives free, set the captives free."

I had absolutely no idea what that meant. Nor did I have a clue as to what I was supposed to do or where I was supposed to go, to **be able to** "SET THE CAPTIVES FREE". My first inclination was to run from that commissioning as fast as I could. Honestly, who wouldn't? But I also knew that based upon the strength of those angels and the force with which God's Spirit had been imparted to me, I didn't have a chance in the world to avoid it, even if I had wanted to. So, recognizing the expected outcome of a potential Jonah-like dash for freedom away from the calling of God, I wisely decided to accept my fate. Sometimes the fear of the Lord is a lifesaver. Literally. Some of you might want to believe that I am stretching the truth or even fabricating this account. For those of you who are skeptical, I would refer you to the Russian prophet, the congregation of that small Russian church and the members of the well-known American ministry who were in Riga that weekend, holding a conference in that church. The church was full of hundreds of people from many different nations, who were all witnesses to the event, which I have just described.

it has been over ten years since that fateful day in Riga, Latvia. In that time I have traveled the world. I have been on the receiving as well as giving side of Christian love and ministration. I have also been on the receiving end of every conceivable, non-sexual malpractice currently being foisted upon Christians in the Body of Christ by the ministers representing it. Some of this abuse was caused by jealousy; most of it was caused by fear. It has opened my eyes to the current state of the church and it has given me a boundless compassion for believers, either new or longer-term, that get caught in the gristmill that is the church at the moment.

To this day, the thing that has kept me going on this quest are the words emphatically spoken by God to me through a Russian prophet and the interpreter kneeling by his side, on the day of my commissioning. This work is the result of that journey toward fulfillment of that commission. I believe it is the reason that God chose me and then called me to "set the captives free".

God Bless You,

S. A. Nitz

Acknowledgements

I would like to thank Rebecca Rhodes, of The Institute of Leadership Development, for her unwavering support and assistance in the creation of the assessment tools and her support of the growth of my personal leadership development. I have learned so much from her that I couldn't even begin to list all of it here. I will be forever grateful, for all of your guidance.

I would also like to acknowledge all of the ministries that have come alongside me during my travels. Dmytro and Iryna Smorzh, the leaders of the Healing Rooms of Ukraine, have been the truest helpers and supporters that a person could wish for. Thank you, Iryna, for helping me to understand the process of how an architect could minister.

Thanks to Gints Grinbergs, and his family, of Atmodas Nams in Riga, Latvia. Thank you for being a support to a foreigner in a foreign nation. I truly appreciate the love and assistance that you gave me on all kinds of levels.

These are just a few of the many ministries that have helped me along the journey. I acknowledge all of the others that I couldn't name in this space and that I may have missed.

The editor and members of MorningStar Journal team, past and present, Emilie Leal, Deb Williams, and Kay Vinci, deserve an acknowledgement for allowing me to present my ideas on the Seven Mountain Message and the rising of the End-Times Army of God in an article to honor the fortieth anniversary of the Seven Mountain Message. Thank you for giving me advice on how to tighten up my writing and how to present my ideas to a totally different audience than I have been used to writing for. Thank you.

Also, Natalie Bruno of ILD deserves a huge round of thanks for her talent and help in creating and producing the chapter illustrations within this book. Thanks also for producing the incredible cover artwork. You are awesome!

Thanks to all of my friends and colleagues who were willing to read the manuscript for this book and to offer feedback on the content, layout, and construction of this work. Proverbs 11:14 states that both wisdom and the guidance of many is necessary for success. Thank you for that guidance.

Finally, I would like to thank all of ministries that I came in contact with on my journeys that gave me a very clear picture of the condition that the Church is currently in. The abuse and mistreatment that I suffered at your hands served only to heighten my awareness of the stark contrast between God's design for the Church, as clearly described in His Word, and the way in which it is currently being done.

Thank you also, to the egotistical and manipulative church leaders that I met along the way. Watching the damage that you inflict upon the flock that you were called to shepherd and protect caused a wellspring of compassion to be birthed in me. It caused a righteous indignation to rise up in me for your suffering sheep and the Body in general. This gave me the strength to continue on the path that The Lord set out before me, so that I could bring His plan for His Kingdom to His Body. Thank you.

Introduction

I am a Reformer/Apostle. That one sentence alone has probably caused a good two-thirds of the people who have this book in their hands and are reading it to jerk. We have all had the experience of being confronted by people who tack the five-fold ministry names onto their names as if they were a title—Apostle so and so, Prophetess so and so, Evangelist so and so, etc. Those are the usual ones. I haven't come across anyone so far, though, who puts the office title of Shepherd or Teacher in front of his or her name. This is probably because those two offices are perceived to be "lesser".

Then we have the people in the Body of Christ who take the positions in the Church and wear those position names like medals of honor—Bishop so and so, Deacon so and so, Elder so and so. Once again, in my opinion, the growth in broadcasting offices and titles experienced in the church in the past years has had very little to do with the function that person has in the Body. More prevalently, it is a reflection of the amount of honor that that person wants to reap from a congregation and from the Church in general. All of it has to do with gaining honor, but not from God.

A funny thing happens, when you have a commission from God. You tend to become very observant. You notice things that others might have overlooked, or things that others consider normal. When The Lord highlights them, however, you recognize that He is trying to show you something. Sometimes it is things that He is not pleased with. The tendency to slap the function of a person in a church as a title or thing of honor before the person's name was the first thing that God showed me, when I began my journey.

Later, when I had seen enough of the different facets of the Body of Christ to recognize the scope of the problems facing it, God revealed the fallacy in that practice. Those offices and positions are not titles; they are job descriptions. Walking around with Bishop in front of your name, as in Bishop Bob Davidson, is the equivalent of stating your name as Carpenter John Jones. Neither one carries more value to God. He sees them all the same. It is the perceived value to man, that causes people to do it.

Once you understand that those positions are job titles and that each "job" has a unique and priceless function within the Body of Christ, you recognize that each and every job is important. There are no "super" jobs or positions. God created His Kingdom in such a way as to require us to work together. No one person has all of the answers. No individual has all of the talents necessary to perform all of the jobs required to keep the Kingdom functioning and to have it function with excellence. The Kingdom was designed as a system of interdependence and each of us has a vital role to play in it.

This was just a first in a series of revelations that I received about the Father's Kingdom structure and how to bring that kingdom into manifestation on Earth. After having been commissioned through a sovereign act of God in a very public way, I had embarked upon a six-year journey to discover why God had commissioned me to "set the captives free" and how I was supposed to accomplish that. At the five-year mark I had a visitation from The Lord at MorningStar ministries. The Lord spoke to me. "Sylvia," He said, "it is time for the Body of Christ to get serious". "It is time for the Body to get serious about discipling the nations" (Isaiah 60:1-4; Matthew 28:19-20 NASB), He added for emphasis. So I asked The Lord what He needed me to do to help the effort.

Then He took me on a journey and showed me all of the places that I had been over the past few years and He reminded me all of the ministries that I had been blessed by. He also brought to remembrance all of the hurts and disappointments that had happened during the process. I realized then, that each of the nurturing and beneficial ministries that I had had the honor of being connected with had a piece of the puzzle of discipleship, a specialization, but none of them had the whole picture. At that point, The Lord downloaded a vision, with a specific strategy to be able to systematically disciple large groups of people. That was the vision. Finding the methodology for birthing the manifestation of that vision then required a lot of prayer and reflective time. The tools necessary to implement the systematic approach to discipleship were born out of that communion time with The Lord.

What you are holding in your hands is the result of a five-year journey to discover the issues facing The Body of Christ and a one-year period of intense prayer and reflection. This book contains revelations about the structure of God's Kingdom, His Kingdom design, and each person's unique role in it. They amazed me, when I received them. They were not the result of an instant download. Instead, I was given additional pieces to the puzzle, when I had successfully placed the previous pieces. In this way the information always remained fresh, and the process remained interesting.

At the end of the one-year process I stood back and was utterly awed at the beauty and majesty of God's design for His Kingdom. As with many things of The Lord, this design was both incredibly complex and utterly simple at the same time. It is complex, in that it requires the cooperation of every member of the Body to complete. At the same time it is inherently simple, because of the clarity of the function of each individual person's part in that design.

The application of the Kingdom design in a person's life requires multiple steps. First, the person must be helped to unload previous hurts and traumas. Then they need to be led towards maturation. This is an ongoing process. Uncovering each person's unique role is the next step to implementing the Kingdom on Earth. After that, each individual needs to grasp the whole systemic structure of the Kingdom. This can happen in the same way that new recruits are educated about the different roles in an army. When the understanding of the system has been established, individuals will then be encouraged to take their place within the specific area in that structure to impact society positively.

The Body is facing the largest harvest in Church history. There have been countless prophecies to this effect. Will we be ready to disciple the millions upon millions of people who are coming into the Body as a result of the next move of The Holy Spirit? Will we be able to take the talents entrusted to us and use them to further His Kingdom on Earth or will we be caught burying them? I am an apostle. In The Kingdom, an apostle's primary function is to bring stuck systems and people into alignment with God's design. This book contains God's plan of how to do just that.

Chapter One – The Army of God

Do You Have a Role in It? – The Longstanding Debate

As long as I can remember, there has been a debate within the Body of Christ as to the exact set of circumstances, which would lead to the return of Jesus and the beginning of the millennium reign of Christ. Up until just recently, the general consensus was that Jesus would triumphantly return and sovereignly establish His reign. Instead of taking action to influence the conditions surrounding them, Christians were led to believe that praying for the Kingdom to come and for Jesus to return was the full extent of their responsibility.

Ministries influenced the body of believers to accept that their part in any good work was a financial one. Believers were called to work in the world and within the world's systems, earn money and then pass this money on to ministries who would then "do" the work of ministry. This attitude led to a form of lethargy and passivity taking hold within the Church. Why expend the energy to fight injustices and change circumstances yourself if you can just pray and hang in there long enough until Jesus shows up? Or, even better, why expend energy yourself if you can pay others to take your responsibility for you?

There is one major problem with this viewpoint: that's not how God works. A whole slew of scriptural verses support the fact that God works in partnership with man and, although He could sovereignly establish His will on Earth, for the most part He chooses to work through people and with people to institute changes in the physical realm. Also, the Word is very clear that every single believer is called to do their part for the Kingdom and every single believer will be held accountable for what they have or haven't done in life. Beginning in Genesis, when God created the Earth, He gave man responsibilities. In Genesis 2:15 we read, " The Lord God took the human and put him in the Garden of Eden to work it and take care of it". God created the Earth, gave abundance and all types of food to the human, but required that human to cultivate that which He had created. Further, in Genesis 2:19-20, we discover that the Lord God had created all of the wild animals and the birds in the sky. He could have, in His sovereignty, given them to mankind with their classifications already established. Instead, "He brought them to the human to see what he would name them; and whatever the human called each living creature, that was its name".

God, the creator, created life and then partnered with mankind in order to ensure that that creation was cared for and tended to. Allowing the first human to name the created beings transferred a sense of ownership and responsibility. This was God's design. He created a world in which His creation could enjoy beauty, prosperity and abundance. He also created it so that mankind had a role to play in the growth and development of that created world. God worked and on the seventh day He rested (Genesis 2:3). He also created mankind in His image. This leads to the question: if we are created in His image and *He* worked, what makes us think that we only have a passive role to play in the redemption scenario?

The creation story was the first instance in which God partnered with mankind to implement things on Earth. It was not the only instance. Further on in Genesis, God partnered with Noah to save specimens of his creation from the flood. Noah was called to build a ship to the specifications from God. Then he and his family were chosen to shepherd and husband those animals until God's cleansing work had been completed on the Earth (Genesis 6-10).

In Genesis 12, God partnered with Abram to provide the foundation for His chosen people, the nation of Israel. Through Abram or Abraham, God would ultimately bring the seed of redemption for the whole world, His Son, Jesus Christ. Because God considered Abraham to be His partner, He was willing to be persuaded to turn away from destroying the cities of Sodom and Gomorrah (Genesis 18:16-33).

God anointed and partnered with Joseph to provide a place of refuge for the budding nation of Israel during a time of drought and famine (Genesis 37-48). Moses was chosen to partner with God in order to rescue the nation of Israel from captivity and to lead it through the desert (Exodus, Leviticus, Numbers, and Deuteronomy). He then partnered with Joshua to bring that same nation into the Promised Land (Joshua). After Israel arrived in the Promised Land, God again partnered with Joshua to help the nation defeat the people occupying that land. It was because of Joshua's obedience to the promptings of God that the city of Jericho was taken. This was only the first of a string of victories provided by God to His people through joint efforts between God and man.

And the partnerships weren't restricted to just the men of mankind. In Judges 4, The Lord partnered with Deborah, the prophet and judge, to bring victory over the army of Sisera and over Sisera himself. In fact, all throughout the Bible, both in the Old and New Testaments, God chose people to partner with in order to manifest His power and His will on Earth. Some of these people were men some were women. All of them, however, were handpicked by God, were created and anointed with the power and skills necessary in order to complete the task chosen for them. God could have sovereignly completed His will on Earth without the help of mankind; He is, after all, God. But He didn't. So the partnership of mankind in the plans of God is crucial to the completion of God's will on Earth. There is no other option. God created the system to function that way.

Somewhere along the way this truth got lost. In addition to that, many Christians have become what I like to call "Dresser Christians". Like a piece of furniture, they have many different drawers. Each one of these drawers contains an aspect of their lives. When they go to work, the work drawer is pulled out and in they go. When they get home from work the work drawer is closed and the family drawer is opened. In this way every single portion of their lives and their existence is compartmentalized.

It might seem like an efficient way to organize life, but it is very deceptive. We are spirit beings. God is a spirit and He created us in His image, therefore we are also spirits. Our physical bodies are simply containers designed to hold our spirits while we are on this Earth. When you separate your life into different aspects you are submitting to your flesh's need for boundaries, structure and control, but essentially, you are putting your spirit into a cage. Many, many Christians' lives function in this way. If you happened to meet them at their job, you would never know that they were Christians. Their Christianity is restricted to church on Sunday, perhaps in a Bible study, an annual church luncheon, or a yearly church bazaar. They give money to charities, but never allow the impact of the Gospel to radically transform their lives or the lives of those around them. They have become passive. Jesus spoke about this lethargical passivity in His letter to the Laodicean church in the book of Revelation (Revelation 3:14-21). In this letter He admonished that this church was neither hot nor cold. Instead, it was lukewarm. Because of this, Jesus promised that He would spew the lukewarm believers out of His mouth.

God created the world and the entire fabric of the universe as a cooperative partnership between God and man. God did the creating part and then passed the stewardship of His creation on to man. Because the job is such a large one, God never meant for man to "go it alone". Throughout history God has always been there to give advice or to make His will clear to those that he chose for specific tasks. After Jesus ascended into Heaven, He sent the Holy Spirit as a teacher to live within believers and to constantly be available to lead and guide us in our daily lives.

This chapter began with the examination of the question as to whether the Kingdom will be manifest after Jesus returns or before He does. The reality is that Jesus cannot return nor manifest the Kingdom until the Church is willing to step into its part in that manifestation. In Luke 17:20-21, Jesus answered a similar question posed to Him by the Pharisees of His time. His response was that the Kingdom was not coming with visible external signs, but that the Kingdom could be found in our midst, or among us.

In a prophetic vision Daniel declared that God's Kingdom was an eternal Kingdom and that that Kingdom would last forever. The rule of God over His Kingdom would exist throughout **all** generations (Daniel 4:3). David, in Psalm 145:13 declares something similar when he states that "Your Kingdom is an everlasting Kingdom, and Your dominion endures through all generations...For Your Kingdom is an everlasting Kingdom... Again in chapter 7 of the book of Daniel, he declared that the holy people of the Most High would receive the Kingdom and would possess it forever—"yes, forever and ever".

The current lethargic Laodicea church (Western church) has been hiding in its prayer closet waiting passively for Jesus to return and sovereignly implement the Kingdom on Earth, although the scriptures are very clear that we have been carrying the Kingdom inside of us all along. In order to implement the Kingdom on Earth, **God is waiting for us** to "get it" and to "get with it". In cooperation with the leadings and ministrations of the Holy Spirit, each one of us has a part to play in manifesting the Kingdom on Earth within our own spheres of influence.

The Kingdom will not sovereignly appear with Jesus' return. Instead, the Body of Christ will use their entrusted talents and manifest the Kingdom **until** Jesus returns. When we submit every aspect of our lives to His Lordship through the guidance of the Holy Spirit, this will open the door for the manifestation of the Kingdom to take place in society and the dominion of the Kingdom of Heaven will begin to usurp the dominion of the kingdom of the world on Earth. "For the creation waits in eager expectation for the children of God to be revealed. For the creation was subjected to frustration...For the creation itself will be liberated from its bondage to decay and brought into the freedom and glory of the children of God" (Romans 8:19-21).

The Sheep and Goat Nations

Coupled with the discussion as to whether Jesus' Kingdom would be manifest on Earth before Jesus' return or as a result of His return, there is a large difference of opinion within the Body of Christ as to the timing of the judgment of the Earth and its inhabitants. There are three major places in the scriptures, where the circumstances surrounding Jesus' return to Earth are discussed. These can be found in the twenty-fourth and twenty-fifth chapters of Matthew, in Revelation, chapter eleven, with parallel scriptures in Daniel, chapter seven; Mark thirteen and Luke chapter seven. This segment will concentrate upon the verses in Matthew and the corresponding verses in Mark and Luke.

To prepare the disciples for His impending death, crucifixion, and resurrection, Jesus had a conversation with them on the Mount of Olives (Matthew 24, 25). It is important to realize that this information was given in private. Jesus was "teaching the teachers". These teachers would then take this message and inform the wider masses upon Jesus' death. It was an intimate time of question and answer. During this discussion, Jesus, through parables as well as direct answers, sought to help his chosen messengers understand the concept of the Kingdom and the events leading up to its complete and final implementation on the Earth.

Often, when studying scripture, there are texts, which seemingly contradict each other. Diametrically opposed concepts are put side by side and the reader is supposed to accept them both as the truth. Generally speaking, these contradictory texts can be viewed in a "both and" relationship, where the normal tendency is to see them as "either or". Let me give an example. In Matthew 24:36, Jesus tells His disciples that The Father alone knows the day and hour of His return. Additionally, He gives a warning that many would try to deceive them into believing that He had already returned (Matthew 24: 23-25). At the same time, Jesus listed a number of signs, economic, and geopolitical events that would herald His return. He also warned them that they were to be vigilant in looking for the signs and signals in order to recognize His eminent return. This would truly cause anyone to scratch his or her head in confusion.

Which is it? Does one trust in the text that tells us only God knows? This leads to a carefree/careless lifestyle in which anything goes. It also generates a type of self-enforced oblivion to Jesus' impending return. Or should one scan the newspapers and television news broadcasts looking for the signs of His impending return. This leads to a life in which long-term decisions and life planning are put on hold. The person would end up living one day at a time, never building anything of lasting value or which could be passed down to another generation.

The answer to this question is in Matthew 24: 42-44, where Jesus explained that the faithful and wise servant would be the one who kept watch and faithfully fulfilled the duties that The Master had entrusted him with. This was further illustrated in two of the most well known parables in the Bible: The Parable of the Ten Virgins, and The Parable of the Talents. In both parables, people are entrusted with tasks and told to fulfill them in the absence of their Master. When the Master returned, He found that some of them were faithful to fulfill their tasks and others not. Those that did their Master's will were rewarded; the others lost their reward and were even punished for their unfaithfulness. So the believer is called to dwell in a permanent state of anticipation, expecting the arrival of the King but at the same time working diligently on the task that has been set before him or her. And this responsibility is not placed upon the individual believer alone.

In Matthew 25: 31-46, Jesus describes His return and the judgment of the nations/peoples of the Earth that will take place. In verse 32, Jesus declares that He will separate the nations that are gathered before Him by putting those righteous nations/peoples on His right and the unrighteous nations/peoples on His left. The ones on His right will be the sheep nations/peoples and the ones on His left will be the goat nations/peoples. This takes the individual responsibility talked about in the other parables to a whole other level.

So not only will a person be individually responsible for their own actions and whether or not they were diligent to do their Master's bidding in His absence, whole nations and people groups will be called to stand before Jesus and be judged according to their collective actions. This is something that is seldom talked about in sermons. According to Matthew 24:31, the faithful will have already been raptured out of the Earth at this point. Those that are left on the Earth when Jesus returns will be judged according to both their individual actions and the actions of the nations that they belong to. Once again, this is a both/and situation. With this insight comes an extra level of responsibility on the faithful believer and follower of Jesus.

Before Jesus ascended into heaven, He gave a directive to His disciples, often called the "Great Commission". Within this directive is the task to the believer to "make disciples of all nations" (Matthew 28:19). The interesting thing about this oft-quoted verse is that the second half of the directive is almost never quoted, "and teach them to obey everything I have commanded you" (Matthew 28:20). The majority of Christians know that they are supposed to go into the world, teach people about Jesus and baptize them in the name of the Father, Son and Holy Spirit. They also know that at the end of the verse Jesus promised that He would always be with believers "unto the very end of the age".

What got lost in the two millennium of teaching on the subject is that it is the believer's responsibility to disciple **nations**. And part of that discipleship program is to teach nations to **obey** Jesus' commandments. Not only is it necessary to disciple individuals, the mandate from Jesus makes it very clear that believers are responsible for making sure that nations know what Jesus' commandments were. And they are equally responsible for making sure that the nations function according to the guiding principles set out through Jesus' commandments.

When the master returns, will He find His followers being faithful to complete the task entrusted to them? Many will think that they have been being obedient, but will have missed the mark. Ultimately, many will claim to have been very holy performing miracles in His name and doing all sorts of "church-like" activities. Jesus was very clear that His response would be to declare that He never knew them and that they would then be assigned a place where there would be weeping and gnashing of teeth (Matthew 7:13, 7:21; Luke 6:46, 13:22-30). Be sure to go through the narrow door.

Biblical Prophecies

One of the amazing things about The Bible is that it is a living document. Not only does it describe history and historical events, it gives us principles by which to design and manage our daily lives. It is also a work that provides a snapshot of future events and gives the reader vital information with which to plan.

The Bible is a book, which includes the blueprint of the Earth and humanity: past, present, and future. Because of this, any major work of God destined to affect the Church and impact the world must have some mention in scriptures. In fact, there are many scriptural verses that describe the Body of Christ rising up to impact society in all aspects and shifting the way things are done from a "worldly" way to a way based upon the teachings of Christ. The book of Daniel is most often cited as a source for scriptural "back-up".

In the second chapter of the Book of Daniel, Daniel was called before King Nebuchadnezzar to interpret the king's dream. Daniel described the dream and then interpreted it. The dream includes the vision of a statue in the shape of a man, with a head of gold, chest and arms made of silver, belly and thighs of bronze, legs of iron and feet partly of iron and partly of clay. These different materials were analogies for different empires. In verses 34 and 35 Daniel describes the process by which the kingdom of the world will be converted to the Kingdom of Heaven on Earth. In Nebuchadnezzar's dream, a cut piece of rock destroyed and then pulverized the statue. The dust of the statue was then blown away by the wind leaving no trace. Finally the rock expanded, grew and became a huge mountain that ultimately filled and dominated the whole Earth (Daniel 2:34-35).

The interpretation of the dream followed in Daniel 2, verses 37 to 45. The key passage can be found in verse 44 where Daniel explains that in the time of the last days' kings God would set up a kingdom on Earth that would never be destroyed or left to another people other than His own. That kingdom would crush all "worldly" kingdoms and bring them to an end. It would also endure forever. It can be rightly interpreted that a struggle is necessary for God's Kingdom on Earth to usurp the world's kingdom, or way of reigning. It also becomes abundantly clear that the establishment of God's Kingdom on Earth is to take place in the midst of the existing world system of governance. Nowhere in this text does Daniel suggest that there is an immediate replacement of the one system for the other.

There are many other verses that deal with the coming Kingdom of God on Earth. Among these are Isaiah 11:9, Isaiah 2:2 and Micah 4:1. All of these verses refer to the coming Kingdom as a mountain. These scriptures will be discussed at length in Chapter Three. In addition to the oft-quoted scriptures noted here, there are other relevant scriptures that are seldom cited. The Old Testament book of Joel offers insight into the movement of an End Times army of God which will take dominion over everything and every system on the Earth.

In Joel 2 the scripture states that:
"Like dawn spreading across the mountains a large and mighty army comes,
such as never was in ancient times nor ever will be in ages to come.
3Before them fire devours, behind them a flame blazes. Before them the land is like the Garden of Eden, behind them, a desert waste—nothing escapes them.
4They have the appearance of horses; they gallop along like cavalry.
5With a noise like that of chariots they leap over the mountaintops, like a crackling fire consuming stubble, like a mighty army drawn up for battle.
6At the sight of them, nations are in anguish; every face turns pale.
7They charge like warriors; they scale walls like soldiers. They all march in line, not swerving from their course.

Joel describes a movement of God like an invading army scaling walls and consuming all stubble in its path. There will be no realm of the natural that is safe from its power and its effect, because the members of this army will overrun the cities and climb into houses. Even the private realms of people's lives are subject to the effects of this army because they will enter like thieves through the windows (verse 9). However, as great as the power of this End-Times army will be, and as mighty as the display of this power will be, the single most important quality of its members will be their obedience to the Lord and His commands (verse 11). The Old Testament prophets had prophetic dreams and visions. Some, like Daniel, interpreted prophetic dreams and visions about the Kingdom. Jesus, the greatest prophet of them all, used parables. One of the most applicable to this discussion is the Parable of the Weeds or the Parable of the Wheat and the Tares, found in Matthew 13:24-30.

In these verses, Jesus describes the Kingdom as a field of wheat planted by the owner of an estate. When the wheat began to grow, the servants of the owner discovered that there were weeds growing up between the stalks of wheat. Wanting to help their master, the servants suggested weeding out the unwanted plants. The master, on the other hand, declared that the weeds were to be left in the field to grow up next to the wheat. At harvest time the weeds were then to be harvested first and burned and the wheat was to be harvested afterwards and brought into the barn.

The explanation follows in verses 36-43. The field, according to Jesus, is the world. The good seed, sown by Jesus, are the people of the Kingdom. The weeds represent the people who follow and do the works of the enemy.

Verses 40 and 41 provide a clear explanation of the End-Times process, to take place. According to Jesus, at the end of the age, He will send His angels to first weed out everything in the Kingdom that causes sin and all who do evil. These will be gradually harvested and burned up so that the Kingdom people remaining will shine with increasing brightness. These verses show that the process will be gradual, with the Kingdom people standing next to the people of the enemy, until the angels ultimately remove and destroy them.

Modern Prophetic Words

God does not do anything, until he first reveals it to His prophets (Amos 3:7). Prophets did not die out in Old Testament times. There are many today, who also have a prophetic calling on their lives. Therefore, any prophetic word found in the Bible will find more and more voices heralding it, as the time for its fulfillment draws near. This is also true of prophetic words proclaiming the implementation of the Kingdom on Earth.

In *The Call* by Rick Joyner, senior pastor of MorningStar Ministries, he recalls a vision of an army, which echoes the description of the End Times army of the Lord written about in Joel Chapter 2.

"As the soldiers marched, their armor and weapons flashed in the sun like lightning, and the flapping of the banners and the tread of their feet sounded like rolling thunder. I did not think that the Earth had ever witnessed anything like this before. Then I was close enough to see their faces—male and female, old and young from every race. There was a fierce resolution on their faces, yet they did not seem tense. War was in the air, but in the ranks I could sense such a profound peace that I knew that not a single one feared the battle to which they were marching." The Call, Rick Joyner, MorningStar Publications, 1999, pp. 137-138.

The word of the Lord released to Lana Vawser, Australian Prophetic Council, Brisbane, Australia, directed toward the Church in the United States of America and published on Elijah List on June 27th, 2015, states that:

"I am raising up an army in the UNITED STATES OF AMERICA, that will not be swayed by what they see and will not give up. In the midst of areas of darkness in the nation, I am raising up My Church. This is

*THE GREATEST HOUR for My people in the UNITED STATES OF
AMERICA. IN AMONGST the darkness, I am positioning My people as
they stay close to Me, to SHINE like never before.*
*As more darkness has seemingly begun to fall upon the nation, My
Church is about to rise and shine (Isaiah 60) like NEVER BEFORE
and SHOW the nation of the United States what VICTORY LOOKS
LIKE. An army not moved by victory in the 'NATURAL' but moving
from a place of ASSURED CONTINUAL VICTORY by standing
STRONG in Me.*
*Church of America, this is your FINEST HOUR!!!! It's time to ARISE.
Some of the greatest demonstrations of My power and My love are
going to be seen in this day. DO NOT give up hope. For in the
darkness, you will find your FINEST HOUR. It is always darkest
before the dawn. The dawn of the sons and daughters of glory arising
to show the nation what TRUE VICTORY looks like."*

The past few years have seen an increase in prophetic words about the
Kingdom of God, the rise of an End-Times army of God, the overthrow of
the world's system by Kingdom people and other related topics. These two
prophetic words are only representative of many, many others. In fact, nearly
every leading prophetic voice in the Church today has issued some prophetic
word covering one or more of these topics. As the Kingdom begins to
manifest in greater authority on the Earth and, as the "tares" begin to be
weeded out by the angels, these prophetic voices will get stronger and louder.

Chapter Two – Jesus and the Kingdom

Most people, when asked about the primary lesson taught by Jesus, will answer "love". While love was an important part of His message, it is overshadowed many times over by the greatest and most prevalent lesson that He preached and communicated about.

In doing some research into the subject I discovered a passage in the Zondervan Pictorial Encyclopedia of the Bible:

> *"The word 'kingdom' is found fifty-five times in Matthew; twenty times in Mark, forty-six times in Luke and five times in John. When allowance is made for the use of the word to refer to secular kingdoms and for parallel verses of the same sayings of Jesus, the phrase 'the Kingdom of God' and equivalent expressions (e.g., 'Kingdom of Heaven', 'His Kingdom') occurs about eighty times…These statistics show the great importance of the concept in the teachings of Jesus… There can, therefore, be little doubt that the phrase 'the Kingdom of God' expresses the main theme of His teaching"*
> *(Vol. III, Zondervan, Grand Rapids, 1976, p. 804).*

This was a revelation to me. Love, loving, unconditional love, etc., was a major part of Jesus' message, this is true. The idea, however, was that the love is to be used as a tool to further something else…The Kingdom. Somehow and somewhere along the way, the teachings of Jesus on the Kingdom as the goal of Christian lives, and love as a manifestation of the Kingdom, got truncated to a message of love as the goal. Since I can imagine that this idea is shocking to some of you, we'll spend some time here examining it.

Jesus and The Kingdom Message

Even before Jesus arrived on the scene in ancient Israel, the Kingdom was being preached. John the Baptist spent his days calling for repentance, "because the Kingdom of Heaven has come near" (Matthew 3:2). He preached in the desert, calling Jews to turn from their wicked ways, since a shift was about to take place within the world and he had the task of "preparing the way" for the king of the new kingdom to arrive (Isaiah 40:3, Matthew 3:3).

In ancient Israel, the Jews had been being primed for the coming of the Messiah for many millennia. The old-Testament prophets spoke of the coming of the King and the establishment of the Kingdom of God, so Jews educated in the Torah were aware of these prophecies. Because of the occupation of the country through the Romans, the people's desire for and anticipation of the coming of the King caused them to expect a military and governmental leader. The military, governmental and religious hierarchical structures of the day created an expectation of a top-down leader and leadership. It was the standard governance form of the day. In fact, it was the only form of guidance widely available at that time. All of these expectations formed the environment into which Jesus was born. When He failed to meet those expectations, the troubles began.

Jesus' ministry actually began after His forty-day sojourn in the desert. When He returned to civilization, He went and lived in Capernaum where He began to preach. His first recorded sermon was "Repent, for the Kingdom of Heaven has come near" (Matthew 4:17). This began a ministry of miracles, signs, wonders, preaching, and teaching leading up to His persecution, death on the Cross, and resurrection.

The message He taught never really waivered from the central theme of "Kingdom come near" and He often used parables to highlight aspects of the Kingdom. Depending upon the method of counting, the number of these parables can vary. However, most credible sources list sixty separate parables comparing various characteristics of the Kingdom or Kingdom life. In fact, the overwhelming majority of the parables taught by Jesus were introduced with the preface, "the Kingdom of Heaven is like…" (Matthew 13:24, 31, 33, 44, 45 and 47).

When asked by His disciples why He spoke in parables (so that the majority could not understand), Jesus answered, "Because the knowledge of the secrets of the Kingdom of Heaven has been given to you, but not to them" (Matthew 13:11). He spoke in parables, so that only those who had "eyes to see and ears to hear" (Matthew 13:13-17) would understand. Taken together, Jesus' parables offer insight into the character of the Kingdom, the character of the King, and the character of the King's subjects. To the person seeking to become a subject of the Kingdom, or seeking to help others do the same, understanding the teachings of Jesus on the Kingdom is not enough. In fact, Jesus was very clear about the consequences for those who refused to subject themselves to the Kingdom, and the Kingdom way of doing things. Being a Kingdom subject requires that one submits or "subjects" himself to the laws, rules, regulations of the Kingdom and the sovereignty of the King. Jesus was clear on this requirement, when He asked "why do you call me Lord, Lord and do not do what I say?" (Luke 6:46). Even more telling was His warning that not everyone who called Him Lord would enter the Kingdom (Matthew 7: 21-23).

The Sermon on the Mount: A Love Message?

Jesus' most famous teaching is commonly known as the "Sermon on the Mount". It can be found in Matthew 5-7 with parallel verses found in Luke 6: 17-49. Cited extensively in Bible teaching, it is most often used to admonish believers to "love". Although the sermon does touch upon how to love and most especially loving one's enemies (Luke 6:27-36; Matthew 5:43-48), the true focus of the teaching is to explain the characteristics of the subjects of the Kingdom to the listeners.

Jesus' first sentence clarifies the purpose of the talk, "Blessed are the poor in spirit, for theirs is the Kingdom of Heaven". This is the King, of the Kingdom, explaining to His future subjects the laws of the Kingdom. And those laws were also given in a pack, just as the Commandments were presented to Moses. God gave Moses the Ten Commandments to distinguish the Israelites from all other people groups on Earth. It was their obedience to the law, which marked their loyalty to God. Through their obedience to the law, other people and people groups could recognize them.

Jesus gave His followers the Beatitudes. But these were not rules of conduct. Instead, these were characteristics, which would describe the followers of Jesus and would highlight the difference between His Kingdom and the kingdom of the world. People would be able to recognize the followers of Jesus, but not by their adherence to a set of rules. They would recognize them through the manifestation of grace upon their lives; the grace brought upon them by a belief in the death, crucifixion and resurrection of Jesus and by the fruit and manifestation to the world of the indwelling of the Holy Spirit within them.

Characteristics of Kingdom Subjects[1]

The primary characteristic of a subject of the Kingdom of God is the recognition of the Lordship of Christ in their life. It is enough for someone to believe in Jesus' sacrifice as the Son of God and Son of Man in order to be saved and receive eternal life, because anyone who calls upon the name of the Lord will be saved (Romans 10:13-14; Acts 2:21, 4:12). It is not, however, enough for someone to simply believe in order to inherit the Kingdom (Matthew 7-21-23; Luke 6:46).

A profession of faith in Jesus must be followed by actions taken based upon obedience to the leadings of the Spirit. By submitting to the King's authority we become citizens of the Kingdom of Heaven (Philippians 3:20). By accepting the fellowship of Jesus' sufferings and by imitating Christ in His submission to the will of the Father we step into the authority reserved for the citizens of the Kingdom. Jesus came to Earth to model for us the Kingdom and its power. Jesus made it clear that He only did what He saw His Father do and only said what He heard His Father say (John 5:19, 12:49). Because of His submission to the promptings and leadings of the Father, Jesus was able to walk in the level of manifestation of miracles, signs and wonders that He did. This characteristic is called being Poor in Spirit.

The second characteristic of subjects of the Kingdom of Heaven is the sorrow that they carry for their own sins as well as the sins of the world. The recognition of the sinful nature of man and the world is the next step in the emptying process that takes place as a person moves from the dominion of the world to the dominion of the Kingdom. Jesus was a man familiar with sorrows and grief (Isaiah 53:3, Matthew 23:37, Luke 19:41, John 11:35). Mourning is a result of a burden of sorrow placed upon the believer by The Holy Spirit.

Characteristics of Kingdom Subjects

- **Poor in Spirit** – Obedient to the leadership of the King
- **Mourn** – Carry a deep sorrow over the condition of the world and of our own sinful nature
- **Meek** – A God controlled life leads to humility, long-suffering, and moderation
- **Hunger and Thirst for Righteousness** – Seek righteousness of Christ, which leads to gratefulness
- **Merciful** – Willing to understand the situations that lead to actions of others
- **Pure in Heart** – Become mature through the cleansing of our hearts by God
- **Peacemakers** – Mediate a reconciliation of others to God and the ways of God
- **Persecuted because of Righteousness** – Willing to endure persecution as a representative of the Kingdom

It is the outward manifestation of conviction working in the life of the believer. When Jesus ascended into Heaven, God sent The Holy Spirit as a helper (John 16:8-11). It is his job to bring this conviction, especially in the areas of sin, righteousness, and judgment. Mourning is the second step in the maturation process, which a believer must go through in order to transition from the world's way of doing things to God's way of doing things.

The third characteristic of Kingdom subjects is meekness. As in mourning, meekness is the outward manifestation of the inner workings of God in our lives. Its attributes include humility, but primarily humility with respect to the person's behavior towards others. A person who exhibits meekness is adept at restraining him or herself in order to allow room for others. The meek are patient under affliction and suffering. They are teachable. The meek are those that do not have to stand in the spotlight. They are willing to place others before themselves. They display humility, but this humility is not necessarily directed toward them. Humility towards oneself is a humility, which says, "I am not that important, my skills are not better than others". Humility toward oneself in an unhealthy form can be self-depreciating. Meekness is a humility directed towards others. It is stepping back in order to allow others to step forward, to shine, to grow and to become more than they currently are.

The primary manifestation of meekness in Kingdom subjects is their habit of giving God the honor and glory for things that happen in their lives. As God directed subjects, achievements are simply the result of obedience to the promptings and leadings of the Spirit of God. As such, these achievements are nothing that an individual could claim as the fruit of their own efforts. The meekness displayed by a Kingdom subject acknowledges the efforts of others as critical to the success of an undertaking while, at the same time, realizing that one's own efforts were simply the result of obedience to God. Having gone through a transformation of character and the breaking of an ego to the point that meekness emerges, the next characteristic of a Kingdom subject will become evident.

People at this level of maturation and discipleship begin to hunger and thirst after righteousness. This longing will manifest in two forms – the internal and the external. Kingdom subjects will seek to be and do right. That is, they will begin to remove all things from their lives that are perceived to be "wrong" and "sinful". Generally speaking, this process begins with a period of self-reflection and then self-effort. When the person realizes that nothing that he or she can do will bring the results longed for, recognition of the full scope of grace brought about through the sacrifice of Jesus begins to emerge. The result of this realization is an even greater level of humility and extreme gratitude. The external manifestation of the hunger and thirst for righteousness is a push to remove things that are sinful and wrong from one's environment. At this point, the Kingdom subject will begin to work to change things in the world that are perceived to be at odds with the values and norms as written in The Bible. Directed in critique towards people and circumstances, it could be mistaken for a religious spirit. Because the realization has been reached that it is impossible for a human to achieve the righteousness of God through self-effort, this external push will result in efforts to bring people and systems into righteousness by confronting them with Jesus.

Kingdom subjects with the fifth characteristic are merciful. Because they have realized that righteousness cannot be obtained through self-effort and that it is only through the grace allotted through the sacrifice of Jesus upon the Cross-, they understand that all sin is a result of a regression into thoughts and actions dominated by carnality. Although the born-again spirit of a person is perfect and free of sin, the flesh is subject to corruption through wrong thoughts and wrong handlings based upon those thoughts. Realizing this leads to the insight that all people have sinned (Romans 3:23) and can sin. Being merciful and understanding towards others is the outward manifestation of this level of maturity. People who are merciful extend the grace and mercy they have encountered in Jesus to others. They seek to understand the circumstances that cause someone to fall into those situations. Merciful people can walk a mile in someone else's shoes.

The sixth characteristic of subjects of the Kingdom of God is purity of heart that results from a washing. The heart is the throne of the spirit and the center of a person. When God works in a person's life, He begins from the inside out. The Holy Spirit is sent to work in a person's life and to cleanse that person from the effects of a life lived in a sinful and fallen world. Inner wounds are healed and wholeness is the ultimate result (Psalm 51:10-12). This cleansing and healing process is very important to God (Proverbs 4:23). The broken and wounded soul is ministered to by the Holy Spirit in a process designed ultimately to match the condition of the soul and the body to the condition of the righteous born-again Spirit of a person (Psalm 147:3). The pure in heart become the pure in heart through the grace of God extended into their lives. They do not achieve it by works (Ephesians 2:8-9).

Kingdom subjects are peacemakers. This is the seventh characteristic. All of these characteristics are related and also progressive. This means that it is not possible to manifest the characteristic of being a peacemaker, until hearts have been cleansed. The peacemaker becomes a peacemaker, because he or she is at peace. This peace cannot be achieved through external workings. Instead it is the manifestation of a "right" relationship with God (Romans 5:1). This right standing with God will then lead to the person experiencing the peace of God (Philippians 4:7). There is no peace outside of Jesus Christ (Isaiah 48:22). Because only through the acceptance of the sacrifice of Jesus for our sins, can we be brought back into relationship with a Holy God. God is a God of peace (Philippians 4:9). And having experienced the peace that comes from a submission to the Prince of Peace (Isaiah 9:6) a Kingdom subject will then seek to live at peace with all others (Romans 12:18).

Not only that, but the Kingdom subject will then begin to spread the message of peace through the redemptive gift. The peacemaking activities of a peacemaker are generated from an internal conviction that the only true way to manifest peace on the Earth is by helping people, regions, cities, nations and the world, to make peace with God (Romans 15:13). It is not by works of man that a lasting peace is achieved, but rather, it is through a right relationship with God the Father that peace is achieved. Once again, this happens first internally, and then manifests externally.

The first seven characteristics of a Kingdom subject come about through the inner transformation and healing of a person. They are interrelated, successive, and progressive. The eighth characteristic comes about through the outward manifestation of the first seven, commonly known as "The Beatitudes". The Beatitudes are characteristics, which are totally contrary to the normal human condition. They are characteristics sought by Christians and draw a line of sharp distinction between believers and non-believers.

People mistrust things that are different. The normal reaction to mistrusted things is to keep a great distance between you and it or to try to change whatever it is into something more comfortable and familiar. This is called persecution. Jesus, who came to Earth to model a Kingdom lifestyle, lived a life so anti-establishment that that establishment sought any means possible to keep Him in check. When that didn't work, the final solution to the problem was to unjustly accuse Him and then to murder Him on the Cross. Jesus was the rock of offense (Isaiah 8:14, Romans 9:33, I Peter 2:8).

The first seven Beatitudes mark a progression in the discipleship and maturity of a believer. They also mark the characteristics of a Kingdom subject. The more the first seven of these characteristics manifest, the more the person becomes like Jesus. Having become more like Jesus, a Kingdom subject can count on the world reacting to him or her like it did to Jesus. Persecution is the result of a believer manifesting the characteristics of Jesus.

If you aren't being persecuted by the world, by people, or even by the "establishment" then you, quite simply, aren't manifesting enough of the characteristics of Jesus to affect the world, the church, or any other realm that you are working in. A willingness to endure persecution and suffering, as a representative of the Kingdom and of its King, is the eighth characteristic of a Kingdom subject.

Characteristics of the Kingdom

Jesus taught His disciples to pray, "Your Kingdom come, Your Will be done on Earth as it is in Heaven" (Matthew 6:10). In church culture, this has become so commonplace that most people have never stopped to ponder what, exactly, they have been praying for.

Characteristics of the Kingdom

- The Kingdom is within the subjects
- The Kingdom exists parallel to the world
- Subjects are placed in strategic places in the Kingdom
- It manifests when the obedient subjects faithfully grow and use their talents
- The King sends angels to begin to weed out the subjects of darkness
- The Kingdom begins to manifest in greater and greater measure, as the enemy's subjects are removed from their positions
- The expansion of the Kingdom causes light to usurp the darkness
- The Subjects of the King are rewarded

When asked by the Pharisees when the Kingdom of God was coming and how it was supposed to manifest, Jesus explained to them that they needed to stop looking externally for signs that the Kingdom had arrived. Instead, Jesus made it very clear that the Kingdom was in their midst, or, in different words, the Kingdom was already there (Luke 17:20-21). Other scriptures make it clear that the Kingdom has always been among us, because it is an eternal Kingdom (Psalm 145:13). The Kingdom endures from generation to generation, in fact, for all generations (Daniel 4:3).

These scriptures then raise another question. Believers are told to pray, "Your Kingdom come…on Earth". So either Jesus got it wrong, or we haven't understood it correctly. I think that we can all agree that it is the second of the two options. Jesus taught that we are to stop looking for the outward manifestation of the Kingdom and that we should look to ourselves, because the Kingdom is in our midst. The second portion of that prayer tells us how the Kingdom is to manifest in our midst. "Your Will be done on Earth as it is in Heaven" (Matthew 6:10). The Kingdom will manifest on Earth, when believers receive it and submit to God in everything that they do. The Kingdom is within the subjects, because, as born-again believers, they have the King indwelling in their spirits. The Kingdom truly is in the midst, or within, the believers. They simply need to receive that Kingdom and subject themselves to the rule of the King (Daniel 7:18).

Jesus taught in parables. The most prevalent theme of those parables was the Kingdom. In twenty different stories, Jesus explained the Kingdom. He used the various narratives to highlight different aspects of the Kingdom and how the Kingdom functioned. Studying and contrasting the various parables brings clarity as to the role that each believer plays in bringing God's Kingdom to Earth. As we have learned, the first and primary characteristic of the Kingdom is that the seed of it is placed in every born-again believer when they accept Christ as their Savior and Lord. What happens after that is a matter of free will. We do not currently see much of the manifestation of the Kingdom on Earth, because believers are ignorant about the role that they have to play in that manifestation process.

The second major characteristic of the Kingdom is that it exists parallel to the world's system of governance. Jesus illustrated this quality in four of His parables. The primary example stems from the Parable of the Weeds

(Matthew 13:24-29) with the explanation of that parable following (Matthew 13:37-43). In this parable, Jesus explains that God (the owner) sows seeds in a field (the world). The seeds sown are the people of the Kingdom. At night, the enemy (devil) comes and sows his own seeds in the field. The seeds of the devil are people who are obedient to the enemy. These people are not necessarily Satan worshipers. They can simply be people (even believers) that refuse to submit to the lordship and leadership of the King.

Rebellion is as witchcraft (1 Samuel 15:23) and rebellion against God means that you automatically belong in the enemy's camp. There is no neutral territory. You are either the one, or the other. The Parable of the Talents (Matthew 25:14-30) and the parallel Parable of the Minas (Luke 19:11-27) make this point clear. A believer can only become a subject of the Kingdom and begin to manifest the Kingdom on Earth, when that person is willing to submit to the King. Following one's own desires or whims will automatically put a person squarely on the side of the enemy. A person cannot follow the flesh and fleshly desires and claim to be a subject of the Kingdom. The two are mutually exclusive.

This leads to the third feature of the Kingdom. Since the King is the one who sows the seed in His field (the world), He does that strategically. The King's subjects are specifically created to fulfill a unique role and position in the Kingdom. Therefore, He places them purposefully, in order to best utilize the talents that they were created with. Here again, the Parable of the Talents illustrates this point, as the master distributed his talents to his servants, to the degree that they were able to handle them. The master gave five to the one servant, two to the next and one to the third. This unequal distribution occurred, because the servants had proven themselves before and the master knew which one of the servants had the greatest ability. He distributed the duties in response to the ability of each of his servants. He will never give out more responsibility, than a person can handle, or was created for.

In addition to that, God is also fair and willing to give everyone an equal chance. In the parable of the Minas, the king distributed his Minas equally. He called ten servants and gave each servant one Mina. Once again, there were three different results achieved by the servants. The first type of servant earned an additional ten Minas for the one he was given. This is a 1000% return on the investment. The second type of servant earned an additional five

Minas. This is a 500% return on the investment. The last type of servant went and hid the Mina and returned it.

Having been created with specific gifts and having been given those gifts for a specific purpose, it is then up to the person with those gifts to grow them and use them to expand and grow the Kingdom. Here, the Parable of the Sower and the Parable of the Mustard Seed offer the perfect illustration of this point (Matthew 13:3-9/Matthew 13:31-32, Mark 4:3-20/Mark 4:30-32, Luke 8:5-15/Luke 13:18-19).

Given the right soil, which is a willing believer, the seed sown can yield one hundred fold, sixty fold or thirty fold. Taking the smallest of the seeds, a mustard seed, when that seed is tended and cared for, it can become the greatest of the herbs in a garden, growing into a tree and offering shelter for the birds. The seed of the Kingdom, planted in the believer and cared for and tended to will end up yielding a harvest for the King. The size of the harvest depends upon the ability of the believer, but it primarily depends upon the willingness of the believer to steward the gifts and talents, that is the seed, given to him or her. The harvest of this faithful stewardship is the expansion of the Kingdom on Earth. This is the fourth distinguishing feature of the Kingdom. Subjects of the Kingdom are called upon to grow and use the talents that were given to them in order to increase the dominion of God's Kingdom on Earth.

This does not necessarily mean that a bloody war ensues with physical casualties, since we do not fight against flesh and blood (Ephesians 6:12). Instead the war is primarily an ideological war and the battles take place primarily in the minds of people. The manifestation in the world occurs, when the internal reality begins to line up with the Word of God and with His way of doing things. People's thoughts change and ultimately they will begin to think and act differently, because of that change in thought process.

Depending upon the mountain or sphere of influence to which one has been called, these differences in thought will lead to the creation of goods and services that serve the population and line up with the values inherent in the Bible. They will be a physical manifestation of God's way of doing things. This is God's Kingdom on Earth.

Thankfully, this effort will not be as strenuous as it might seem to be. As the subjects of the Kingdom grow stronger and stronger, they will begin to expand in influence. Using the seed and plant analogy, they will begin to crowd out the weeds, as they begin to grow. God will support this crowding out process by sending His angels to remove the weeds from His field. The weeds are the enemy's subjects and the field is the world. The Parable of the Weeds, The Parable of the Net, and the Plants of the Father illustrate this (Matthew 13:24-29, Matthew 13:47-50, Matthew 15:13-14).

As we look out into the world, we can see this weeding-process taking place all around us. It seems that the NEWS is full of stories of leaked information exposing corrupt officials. This is an outward sign that the Lord has already begun to send His angels to remove the weeds. As more and more evil and darkness is exposed, the responsibility of the sons and daughters, the Kingdom subjects, is to step into those places surrendered by the servants of the enemy (Romans 8:18-20). This shift is the manifestation on Earth of the fifth Kingdom characteristic.

The sixth characteristic of the Kingdom is an extension of the fifth. As the Kingdom servants begin to step into and expand their influence in the areas/mountains that they have been positioned in, the Kingdom will begin to usurp the world's way of doing things. The light will become greater and greater and the darkness will be pushed away. The son's and daughters of God will shine like a city on a hill. Their light will not be hid under a basket (Matthew 5:14-16). The Kingdom will begin to shine more and more brightly into the darkness and the darkness will have to flee (John 12:46).

The church has given the impression, through teachings, that this process will be an instant one. Jesus would return and then, POOF, His Kingdom would be established on Earth. Believers wouldn't be called to do anything except hide in their prayer closets, as the world gets darker, and keep praying for the process to be over with. In the best case, they would pray that the process be over with quickly.

Jesus never taught this. Instead, through His parables, He made it very clear that the coming of the Kingdom is a process. That process is a cooperative effort between God and man. God will do His part, when we have stepped up to do ours. The most clear scriptural text declares that, "…and there were loud voices in heaven, which said: "The kingdom of the world **has become** the Kingdom of our Lord and of His Messiah, and he will reign for ever and ever" (Revelation 11:15). This is the seventh characteristic of the Kingdom.

The eighth characteristic will manifest as a result of the rise of the previous seven. God is a God of recompense (Isaiah 61:7). The faithful servants can expect to be rewarded for their service to the King. They will be able to hear the words, "Well done, good and faithful servant" (Isaiah 54:17, Psalm 35:27, Matthew 25:21-23, Mark 10:29, Luke 18:29).

---

[1] http://catholicexchange.com/the-beatitudes-stages-of-christian-development

The
Seven
Mountain
Message

Chapter Three–
The Seven-Mountain Message

Understanding the structure of The Kingdom and how each individual fits into that structure requires starting at the beginning. Most people within the Body of Christ have heard about the Seven Mountain message. Some vocal members of the Body have been great champions of the message. Among them are Lance Wallnau and Johnny Enlow. Lance Wallnau, according to the Kingdom definition, is a Proclaimer. He has made a name for himself traveling the world and teaching about the "Seven Mountains". Along with the teaching aspect of the message, his evangelistic portion has been to animate the Body to step into that mandate.

Johnny Enlow, who is a Revelator, has written a number of books examining aspects of the Seven Mountains. Many of those books offered scriptural parallels to the idea and have served to expand upon the original intent of the mandate. Additional authors, like Os Hillman and Bronwyn O'Brien have also written extensively on the mountains. All four modern carriers of the message have done well in educating people. The missing portion of the message and its modern interpretation has been the practical application. The "what" and "why" of the message has been adequately delivered, but the practical methodology of "how to" has been missing.

The interesting thing about the fact that Johnny Enlow, Lance Wallnau, Os Hillman, and Bronwyn O'Brien from Australia are currently associated with the mandate is that very few people realize that the Seven Mountain Mandate message *did not* originate with them. Although they have been instrumental in spreading the word about the message, they were not the original recipients of the message from God. The root of the message is far deeper and goes further back.

The seed of the word can be traced back thousands of years to the time of the Old Testament prophets. Beginning in the Old Testament book of Joel and continuing in Daniel, Micah and others, the prophets of the Old Testament spoke of the Kingdom. After that, the message was spread through the teachings of Jesus. In fact, the greatest portion of Jesus' teachings had to do with the characteristics of the Kingdom and the Kingdom itself. And, when asked about the best prayer, Jesus taught His disciples to pray specifically for God's Kingdom to be brought to Earth.

In 1975, God simultaneously revealed another aspect of the Kingdom to Bill Bright, Loren Cunningham and Francis Schaeffer. Some time later, having become aware of this, Lance Wallnau and Mark Chironna had a phone conversation in 1985. During this conversation, the original designation of seven "spheres of influence" was changed to the "seven mountains".[1] Although a change in name was not intended in that conversation, it actually solidified the Biblical validity of the message. After that conversation Lance Wallnau picked up the baton to carry that message to a wider audience. Johnny Enlow followed a number of years later with his books. Recently, a number of prophets have been given visions of an End-Times army of God, which would bring forth God's Kingdom on Earth. All of these insights, coupled with those in this book, offer a larger and more accurate picture of His plan for the redemption of the Earth.

The Message Delivered

Bill Bright, the founder of Campus Crusades, and Loren Cunningham, the founder of Youth With a Mission, were both given a specific word at the same time in 1975. Then they were instructed by The Lord to give the message to each other. After having met for lunch in Colorado, while on vacation, they discovered that they had each been given exactly the same message. Later, Francis Schaeffer, founder of the L'Abri community in Switzerland, got a similar word.

They received the directive that in order to significantly impact any nation for Jesus Christ; believers would have to affect the seven spheres, or mountains, of society. Loren Cunningham recalled,

"It was August, 1975. My family and I were up in a little cabin in Colorado. And the Lord had given me that day a list of things I had never thought about before. He said "This is the way to reach America and nations for God. And {He said}, "You have to see them like classrooms or like places that were already there, and go into them with those who are already working in those areas." And I call them

"mind-molders" or "spheres". I got the word "spheres" from II Corinthians 10 where Paul speaks in the New American Standard about the "spheres" he had been called into. And with these spheres there were seven of them, and I'll get to those in a moment. But it was a little later that day, the ranger came up, and he said, "There is a phone call for you back at the ranger's station." So I went back down, about 7 miles, and took the call. It was a mutual friend who said, "Bill Bright and Vonnette are in Colorado at the same time as you are. Would you and Darlene come over and meet with them? They would love to meet with you." So we flew over to Boulder on a private plane of a friend of ours. And as we came in and greeted each other, {we were friends for quite a while}, and I was reaching for my yellow paper that I had written on the day before. And he said, "Loren, I want to show you what God has shown me!" And it was virtually the same list that God had given me the day before. Three weeks later, my wife Darlene had seen Dr. Francis Schaeffer on TV and he had the same list! And so I realized that this was for the body of Christ."[2]

August 2015 marked the fortieth anniversary of the release of the Seven Mountain Mandate to the Body of Christ. Some places, like Almolonga, Guatemala, do exist that have implemented Kingdom principles. However, there has yet to be a single example, anywhere, in which the universal implementation of Biblical principles can be found in all aspects of society. Generally speaking, the word about the mandate has been delivered to the majority of the Body of Christ. Certain churches have tried to disciple their congregations to move into their spheres of influence. However, most of them were missing a plan for practical application. Implementing the Seven Mountain message will usher in the Kingdom of God on Earth and ultimately signal the return of its King. Understanding the Seven Mountain Mandate is key to understanding Kingdom structure and order. When the structure and the purpose of the Kingdom are understood, then it will be possible to implement the plan on a universal scale.

A Rhema Word – Confirmed

Throughout Scripture, when The Lord sent an important word out, it was delivered and validated multiple times. The importance of the message often

corresponded to the number of times the same message was confirmed. Prophetic revelation will always be verified through the written word as well as through other prophets. This way, the accuracy of the testimony is established and the will of God becomes apparent and irrefutable. This is mirrored in the statutes of Jewish law. According to Jewish law, a testimony is only acceptable if the witness is a free man who is not deaf, mentally or morally unsuitable, or too young for Bar Mitzvah. In most cases women are not eligible to testify. A valid eyewitness to an event must have seen the event with his eyes or heard it with his ears. Hearsay is generally inadmissible. Once given, the statement may not be recanted. Finally, a situation is only established as fact by the evidence of two or more witnesses. A single testimony is not admissible. Biblically, a matter is established, if it is seen, heard or experienced by two or more observers (Deuteronomy 17:6 – ESV; 2 Corinthians 13:1 – NAS 1995; Matthew 18:16 – NAS 1995; Deuteronomy 19:15 –
NIV; John 8:17 – NLT).

Although dishonesty exists everywhere, we can be pretty certain that the fear of God was present in the lives of these three men. Additionally, because all three of them received the same word, in different locations, independently of one another, underscores its validity. Biblically, there is a severe price to pay for falsifying words of God or for using words of God for personal gain (Revelation 22:18-19; Deuteronomy 12:32; Proverbs 30:6; Deuteronomy 4:2; and the entire book of Jeremiah 23).

In the case of the Seven Mountain Mandate, three separate leaders in the Body of Christ received an identical word from God at the same time. Loren Cunningham, Bill Bright, and Dr. Francis Schaeffer were the three witnesses required by Jewish Law to establish a matter as factual. Since all three witnesses were men, none of them were mentally or morally unsuitable and all of them were older than the age required for a Bar Mitzvah, this fulfilled the requirements of Jewish Law with respect to the validity of their testimonies. Additionally, all three words were identical, although each was given it separately. None of the accounts was ever recanted.

19Therefore we regard the message of the prophets as confirmed beyond doubt, and you will do well to pay attention to it, as to a lamp that is shining in a gloomy place, until the day dawns and the morning

*star rises in your hearts. **20**First of all, you must understand this: No prophecy in Scripture is a matter of one's own interpretation,*
21*because no prophecy ever originated through a human decision. Instead, men spoke from God as they were carried along by the Holy Spirit.*
2 Peter 1:19-21 ISV

Their collective testimony is considered a factual statement of the will of God, according to Jewish law and according to Biblical mandates. God was so cognizant about the constraints of establishing a matter as fact that He even made it a point to remain within those parameters when delivering His Word to His people. This gives us all the more reason to put our faith in the urgency of this mandate.

The Number Seven

Establishing the validity of a spoken word of God is the first step in embracing and reigniting a collective sense of passion for its fulfillment. The second step is in interpreting the word that was spoken. The Body of Christ is to inhabit and affect seven areas of society in order to turn a nation to The Lord. The number seven is a Biblical number. In the Scriptures it occurs in multiple places. In fact, as a single number, it occurs four hundred and four times in scriptural text. It appears so many times that the online Bible forum, Bible Wheel, comes to the conclusion:

1. *God marked the Bible with the Number Seven because it is the fullness of God's revelation;*

2. *God marked the Bible with the Number Seven because it is His Oath! His Promise! His Covenant; and*

3. *The Number Seven is the heartbeat of Scripture!*
   (http://www.biblewheel.com/Topics/seven.php).

In the Hebrew language, numbers and letters have meaning. Finding the meaning of the number seven requires examining the meaning of the seventh letter of the Hebrew alphabet and drawing a conclusion from that. In Hebrew, Sheva, the seventh letter can mean one of three different things, or a combination of those:

1. Seven;
2. Full, fullness, fill, satisfy, plenty, or satiate; or
3. Oath, to swear, or charge.

The number seven points to the fullness and fulfillment of an oath or a plan. God created the universe, the Earth and everything in it in six days; on the seventh day He rested. His plan for the creation of the universe required a seven. Six days of work, one day of rest (Genesis 2:2).

The plan for the capture of the city of Jericho also included a seven. God told Joshua to march with his armed men around the city once a day for six days. On the seventh day, Joshua and his men were to march around the city seven times. The priests were to blow the trumpets during the march. Upon completion of the seventh round, on that seventh day, the priests were to blow a long blast on the trumpets and the men were to shout. Then the wall would collapse and the city would be theirs (Joshua 6:2-5).

Generally speaking, this part of the story is pretty well known throughout the Body of Christ. What is less known is that Joshua added his own seven to it. In verse 6 we discover that Joshua specifically called for seven priests to carry a total of seven trumpets during the march. There is no mention in the scripture that God specifically required seven priests. Joshua had recognized the importance of the "sevens". As we know, the plan succeeded.

Within the context of the "Seven Mountain" message, the number seven indicates that the word received by the three men in 1975 is the fullness of or the fulfillment of a divine plan. In addition to the scriptural references mentioned, others can also lend further insight: Revelation 1:20, 2:1, 5:6, 8:6, 10:14, 21:9; Numbers 23:1; 2 Chronicles 29:21; Zechariah 3:9 and 4:10; and Psalm 12:6 – NIV states that, "...*the words of the LORD are flawless, like silver purified in a crucible, like gold refined seven times."*

Mountains and Hills

The original message received by Bill Bright, Loren Cunningham and Francis Schaeffer did not contain the word "mountain". The "seven areas" or "seven spheres" got the name "Seven Mountains", by Lance Wallnau and Mark Chironna during a telephone conversation in 1985.

Although without intent on their part, The Holy Spirit was using these two men during that conversation to expand the Body's understanding of The Kingdom revelation received by the three original messengers in 1975. Scripture states that where two or three are gathered together in His name, Jesus is there (Matthew 18:20). Having fulfilled this requirement and in accordance with 2 Peter 1:19-21, the Holy Spirit then influenced and gave utterance to the two men, thereby "carrying them along". A clarification of the original term "areas" was the result of that encounter.

This can be supported through a scriptural study of the word "mountain". There are over five hundred verses in scripture that mention mountains and hills. In order to attempt to find a valid parallel between those texts and the message received by the three original carriers of the message, it is necessary to align the choice of scriptural texts with that message. The "Seven Mountain" Mandate was a prophetic revelation. Therefore, it is wise to begin by looking at what mountains and hills signify in prophetic words documented in The Bible.

In prophetic texts containing the word "mountain", the most common meaning for that term in that context is – *government*. Comparatively then, where mountain would denote world-ruling empires or nations, "hills" mean smaller nations and governments. This denotation becomes very clear when we revisit the second chapter in the book of Daniel, where Daniel was called to interpret the dream of Nebuchadnezzar. Although this story was touched upon in Chapter One, it is worth revisiting more in depth here.

Daniel, having been called before the king to interpret Nebuchadnezzar's dream, proceeded to describe it and then interpreted it. The dream includes the vision of a statue in the shape of a man, with a head of gold, chest and arms made of silver, belly and thighs of bronze, legs of iron and feet partly of iron and partly of clay. These different materials were analogies for different empires. Daniel goes on to describe what happens next.

"While you were watching, a rock was cut out, but not by human hands. It struck the statue on its feet of iron and clay and smashed them. Then the iron, the clay, the bronze, the silver and the gold were all broken to pieces and became like chaff on a threshing floor in the summer. The wind swept them away without leaving a trace. But the rock that struck the statue became a huge mountain and filled the

whole Earth."
Daniel 2:34-35 - NIV.

Daniel interprets the dream in verses 37-45. Then, in verse 44, Daniel describes the rock.

> **"In the time of those kings (emphasis added)**, *the God of heaven will set up a kingdom that will never be destroyed, nor will it be left to another people. It will crush all those kingdoms and bring them to an end, but it will itself endure forever. This is the meaning of the vision of the rock cut out of a mountain, but not by human hands..."* Daniel 2:44-45 - NIV.

The rock described in verse 35 became a mountain that could never be destroyed: an everlasting kingdom. Therefore, in scriptural prophecy, mountains symbolize governments. In this particular scripture, it signifies the Kingdom of God on Earth. In verse 44 and 45, Daniel is describing an End-Times move of God through the faithful disciples and servants of Christ, which will expand and grow to encompass the entire Earth and swallow all of the established human structures and organizations, including, but not limited to, the political structures established by men. Additional scriptural references also support this interpretation. These bear examining in greater detail.

> **"...it shall come to pass in the last days (emphasis added)**, *that the MOUNTAIN of the Lord's house shall be established in the top of the mountains, and shall be exalted above the hills (all of man's governments, great and small); and all nations shall flow unto it. And many people shall go and say, Come ye, and let us go up to the Mountain of the Lord, to the House of the God of Jacob; and He will teach us His ways, and we will walk in His paths: for out of Zion shall go forth the law, and the Word of the Lord from Jerusalem."* Isa.2:2-3 - NIV.

> **"In the last days (emphasis added)** *the mountain of the LORD's temple will be established as the highest of the mountains; it will be exalted above the hills, and peoples will stream to it."* Micah 4:1 - NIV

The major point in these texts is that the mountain, set up by God to have dominion over the Earth systems, is established in the last days. Nowhere in these verses do we see the return of Jesus **before** the implementation of the Kingdom structure on Earth. In fact, these verses point to an End-Times Church becoming aware of its position and authority in the Earth and rising up into that authority to take dominion over the man-made structures and governments operating in the Earth. According to these verses, the mountains, or MOUNTAIN of the Lord are governments or governmental structures set up by God to have dominion over the "hills". The hills are the administrative structures set up by man. And God issued this authority for dominion to mankind during creation. Granted, this authority was lost to the enemy at the fall, but Jesus' sacrifice on the Cross hit the reset button and through his suffering our dominion was restored. Many other Biblical texts allude to this, one of which is the much cited verse of Isaiah 11:9 - NIV,

> *"...They shall not hurt nor destroy in all My Holy Mountain: for the Earth shall be full of the knowledge of the Lord, as the waters cover the sea."*

Most sermons concentrate on the second part of the verse. In fact, many interpretations lean on the understanding that the knowledge of the Lord would cover the Earth when the people of God become full of the knowledge of the Lord. This is partially correct. The Earth will become full of the knowledge of the Lord when the people of God begin to take their place in the world's systems and inhabit their God-ordained places within that structure. Then, they will begin to alter the man-made systems to reflect God's way of doing things and according to Jesus' commands. The result of this effort will be that no one will be "hurt or destroyed" because the systems and structures will become God's Holy Mountain.

---

[1] Chironna, Marc, Broadcast Sermon, God TV Europe, February 2016

[2] http://www.7culturalmountains.org/apps/articles/default.asp?articleid=40087&columnid=4347

The
Seven
Mountain
Rock

Chapter Four - The Seven Mountain Rock

The Seven Mountain Message first received by Bill Bright and Loren Cunningham and ultimately corroborated by the account of Francis Schaeffer was a message that included advice about how to take nations for The Lord. In it, the church was called to step out into seven areas of society instrumental in being able to take a nation for the Kingdom. Many prophetic words, both old and new, tell of a time in which the whole world would bow and acknowledge Jesus as King and Lord (every knee will bow, every tongue confess). Daniel envisioned and came to understand this eventuality, when he was called to interpret a dream given to King Nebuchadnezzar (Daniel 2:34-35).

This dream included a rock, which played the critical role in bringing about a transformation of the world. The role of this rock was to smash the earthly systems of government and governance and to replace them. It was very clear that the rock was pivotal in bringing about this change. Daniel interpreted that rock to be a Kingdom, set up by God.

In order to step into the role of cooperative partner with God in bringing about the transformation of society, called for through the Seven Mountain Message, it is necessary to understand that rock. The rock, in that dream, was the crucial element or tool necessary to bring about that transformation. Gaining a further understanding of the Kingdom by means of the rock is the next step in growing in the understanding necessary to facilitate the transformation from the world to that Kingdom.

The Rock – Jesus and His Teachings

Daniel described a rock in King Nebuchadnezzar's dream (Daniel 2:34-35) that smashed the kingdoms of the Earth and grew to become a huge mountain that filled the entire Earth. Later, in Daniel 2:44-45, he explained that the rock is a Kingdom, which God himself would set up, that would never be destroyed, nor left to others to rule. Ultimately, that Kingdom would crush all of the other kingdoms and bring them to an end. It would endure forever.

Rocks are frequently mentioned in scripture. In fact, there are 176 instances where the singular form "rock" is cited and an additional 48 occurrences of the plural form "rocks". There are three key texts, where the term "rock" occurs, and they are all located in The New Testament. The first of these pivotal texts is found in Matthew 16:18 and Jesus himself uses the term. In that verse, Jesus renames Simon to Peter. The name Peter means rock. Essentially Jesus calls this disciple a rock and continues by saying that this rock was now the foundation of His church. Jesus stated, *"and all the powers of hell will not conquer it." NLT*

It is very interesting to note, that the two "rock" words used in this verse of scripture are not interchangeable. The term that Jesus uses when He renames Peter is Πέτρος, or Pétros in Greek. For you grammar junkies, it is a word that is nominative, masculine and singular. Translated, it means "small stone" or "pebble". In the Greek, Pétros is always used to describe a small stone that someone could hold in their hand and throw. It is usually used to describe a small rock found along a pathway.

In contrast, the term that Jesus uses to describe the stone foundation of His church is πέτρα, or pétra in Greek. Once again, for you grammar junkies, this word is dative, feminine and singular. In the Greek, pétra is always used to describe a large projecting rock, a cliff or a boulder. The two terms are not identical, nor are they interchangeable. Jesus was punning. I am a great fan of puns, so this makes Jesus even more appealing to me. Where Peter is described as a small pebble or an isolated little rock, the foundation of the Church is described as a huge projecting cliff or boulder.

It is beyond me how the church establishment could ever have used the two terms interchangeably, or how they could have used this text to justify establishing a hierarchical church structure with a singular person as its leader. We could take this word study to another level and highlight the fact that Peter is a masculine term and the church foundation is feminine, but following this line of reasoning might stretch the envelope a little too much.

The second fundamental text is I Corinthians 10:4, which reads: *"and all drank the same spiritual drink, for they were drinking from a spiritual rock which followed them; and the rock was Christ."* In this context, the verse is discussing the history of the Israelites in the desert during their 40-year wanderings. The conclusion, which can be drawn from this text, is that "rock" is synonymous with Christ. Here, once again, we discover that the term used for "rock" is πέτρα, or pétra in Greek. Christ is compared to a large boulder or huge protruding cliff and not a small pebble found on the side of a road, which would have been the term Πέτρος, or Pétros.

The final decisive scriptural citation can be found in the parable of the wise and foolish builders in Matthew 7:24-27 and Luke 6:46-49. In this parable, two builders are described. One built on sand, the other built on rock. Finally, during a great storm, the house built upon the rock withstood the great forces working against it. The other house fell apart. Jesus began telling this tale by saying, *"Therefore everyone who hears these words of Mine and acts on them, may be compared to a wise man who built his house on the rock"* *Matthew 7:24*. Here, once again, the term used for rock is the Greek word for protruding cliff/large boulder.

Jesus drew the analogy between His words and acting upon His words to building upon a rock. Jesus was the word made flesh (John 1:14). Therefore, once again, it can be concluded that Jesus, the words of Jesus, and acting on the words of Jesus is equal to a rock, and not just any rock. Jesus made it clear in His use of terminology that building a life based upon His teachings is equivalent to building upon a huge cliff or on a large boulder. There is no mention of the small rock or pebble in these texts. The foundation is solid and massive. Of the 224 Bible verses mentioning rock or rocks, 59 of those equate God with a rock. A few of these verses are: Genesis 49:24, Deuteronomy 32:15, 2 Samuel 23:3, Psalms 42:9, Isaiah 30:29, Habakkuk 1:12, 2 Samuel 22:32, Psalms 18:31, 1 Samuel 2:2, etc.

Therefore, according to scripture, God is a rock, as Jesus is a rock, as are all people who build their lives on the words of Jesus and put them into action. The Church becomes the rock that shatters the world's systems and governments when the believers of Christ begin to build their lives upon the words and teachings of Jesus and act upon them in their daily lives.

The Church Built upon the Rock

The church has been built upon many different things over the course of its history. In the early church days, it was set upon the teachings of the apostles and of the testimony given by these men. After that, a hierarchical church structure removed the responsibility of daily church life from the believer and relocated it into a religious institution. This has been the status quo since.

Certain movements, like the Reformation, sought to shift some of that responsibility and authority back. The weapon used to accomplish this was the Bible. By bringing clarity to the scriptural texts, Martin Luther highlighted the great chasm between the church tradition and the holy text. Translating the ancient text into a commonly used language broke the information monopoly and allowed believers to search the scriptures themselves. Every subsequent church movement has sought to do something similar.

The greatest weapon that believers have is the Word of God. It is sharper than a two-edged sword and it rightly divides between the spirit and the flesh (Hebrews 4:12). It is spirit and life (John 6:63). And it is Jesus (John 1:14). It is only through the diligent study of the Word and its application in our daily lives that we have a chance of influencing our environments and taking territory for the Kingdom. The Church, or Ekklesia, is called to go out of its place of congregation, to go out into the world and to influence the world, by replacing the world's way of doing things with God's way of doing things. The only way a believer is able to know what God's way of doing things is, is to know the Word of God. It is also very important for a believer to have a personal relationship with the Father. This is necessary, so that the Holy Spirit can offer the extra needed advantage, when people are facing decisions.

Only through a thorough knowledge of the Word, will the Church be able to rightly discern between the leadings and promptings of the Holy Spirit and competing directives (my sheep know my voice). Scripturally, God is a rock, Jesus is a rock and Jesus' words and teachings are a rock. People who build their lives upon the teachings of Jesus are building their lives upon a rock/boulder/protruding cliff. Jesus made it very clear that unless a person follows His leading and does what He says, in the decisive moment, He will not know them (why do you call me Lord, Lord/ In that day many will say)

The Church was never meant to be a religious institution offering a ridged structure for conduct and no room for personal identity or freedom. It was never intended to supplant the role of the Holy Spirit in our lives. Instead, the Church, in all of its glorious diversity, in all of its incredible creativity, in all of its manifold forms, was intended to be the Bride of Jesus. The Bride of Jesus, dependent upon His leadership as the head, is the most dynamic, creative, and powerful force ever to walk the Earth. Submitted to the Lordship of Jesus and standing firmly upon the Word, there is nothing that the bride will not be able to accomplish (all things are possible). She is a warrior bride, a conquering bride, and a victorious bride. The wonderful thing is that God never intended for His Son's bride to solely be an object of desire, with no power or authority, and locked away in a harem. Instead, He created her to be a multi-faceted, dominion taking army.

Discipleship - The Key to a Unified Army

At the moment, the Bride of Christ comes nowhere near resembling the warrior army bride that God intended her to be. In order to effectively take the spheres of influence and disciple nations for God, it is imperative that she becomes that bride. The question then remains: How do we get from here to there? As odd as it may seem, in order to disciple nations, we first have to be discipled ourselves.

The first step is to help Christians heal old wounds, in spirit, soul, and body. I had noticed, during my journeys, that each and every conference, book, tape or other material offered some type of help. Generally speaking, they helped in only one specific area. The visitor to the conference did receive help but, at the same time, was left feeling that something was missing. This forced the person to continue searching in the next conference, the next book purchase, the next CD teaching, and the next mission trip, in a never-ending cycle.

As cynical as it may sound, it reminded me of the story of the woman with an issue of blood. She, also, spent all that she had and yet was never truly healed of what ailed her (Luke 8:43-48). A symptom of today's church is that it offers piecemeal solutions to a holistic problem. The woman with the issue of blood eventually, after seventeen years, got the healing that she was so desperate for. She got it, when she skipped the middlemen and went straight to the source of all healing for her healing. She went to Jesus. In order to effectively disciple many people, who will then go on to disciple nations, we must stop forcing people to run around looking for their healing. Instead, we, as the Body of Christ, need to be available to work together to assist them in the process of healing and maturation. When ministries recognize that they each only have a portion of the solution, they will then be mature enough to come together to offer seeking Christians the whole solution.

Once a believer has been assisted in the healing process, he or she will then be ready to learn about and accept their individual identities within the Kingdom structure. Teaching people about their identity in Christ and their position within the army requires tools specifically designed for that purpose. My reconnaissance mission all over the world was followed by a divine connection to Rebecca Rhodes, president of The Institute of Leadership Development, who I met at a conference in Mexico. Under the leading of The Holy Spirit and with her help, I then developed a group of assessment tools. With it, it's possible to help any new or seeking Christian to quickly determine which rank in the army of God he or she has, what the top two spheres of influence are that he or she is called to, the level of development of his or her talents, and the strength of eleven key life skills necessary for a person to have in order to achieve success. These assessments are a tool that promotes understanding and unity in the Church. You can access this tool at: **https://identitypassport.thrivecart.com/kingdom-come-passport/**

Once you know who you were created by God to be and what you were created to do, you need the training and tools to do it. With the tools and skills that you need to step into that role, the next step is the recognition that you are not alone in the Kingdom. Understanding that the Kingdom structure is a structure of interdependence is the next step. Unity in the Army of Christ is the end result of this discipleship process.

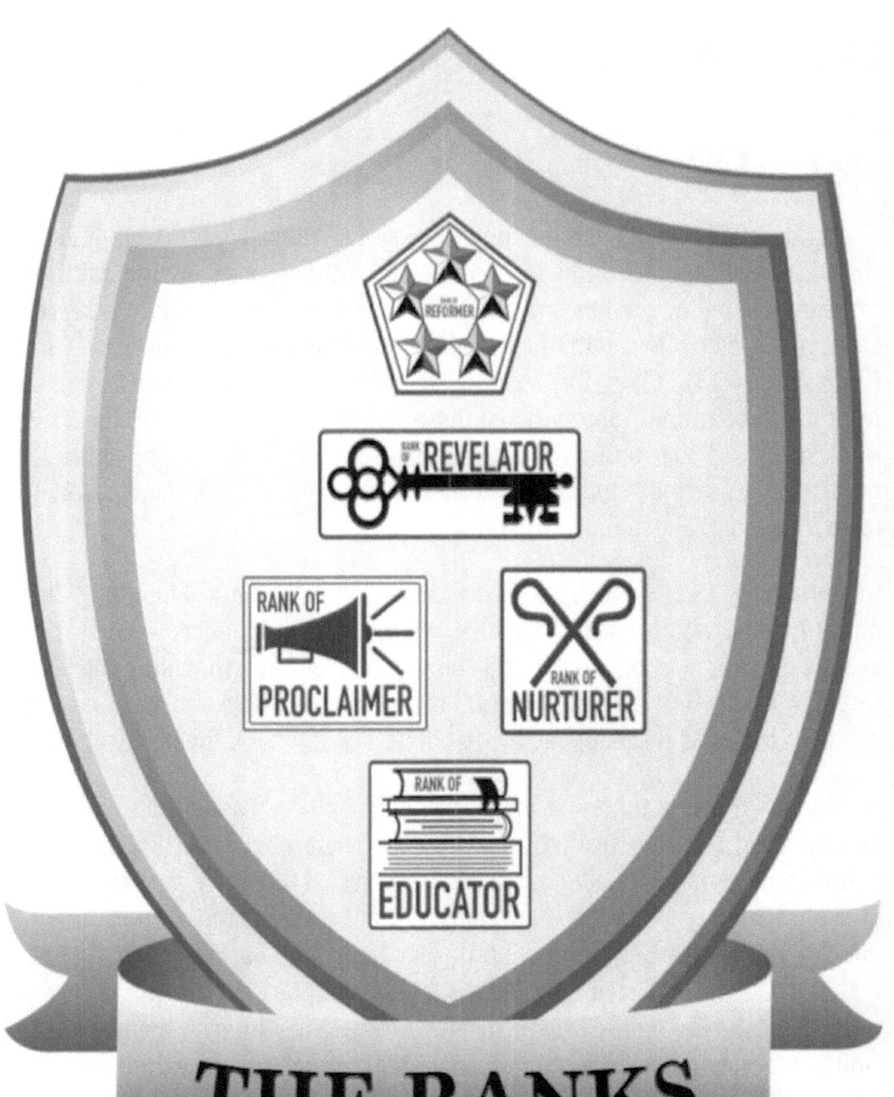
RANK OF
REFORMER
RANK OF REVELATOR
RANK OF PROCLAIMER
RANK OF NURTURER
RANK OF EDUCATOR
THE RANKS

Chapter Five—The Ranks in the Army

The Five-Fold

The Body of Christ has five functions. These functions or roles were given by Christ himself to the Body to support and further unity in the faith and maturity among the members of the faith. Ultimately, these functions serve to support the Body in attaining the whole measure of the fullness of Christ (Ephesians 4:13). Over the span of many years, the organized religious institution of "church" appropriated these functions exclusively for itself. The suggestion was that only "the church" had access to and responsibility for these roles. A serious study of Ephesians 4 uncovers the truth and casts light upon the misunderstanding.

In Ephesians 4:11, the original Greek text reveals the true intention. Christ himself gave some to be apostles, some to be prophets, some to be evangelists, some to be pastors and some to be teachers. So, taking the text at face value, the sum of the "some(s)" must equal a whole. There is no extra category for those that supposedly do not belong to one of the designations.

Additionally, at the time that the original Greek text was written, there was no organized religious institution of church. Therefore, these functions must be inherent in and available to the entire Body of Christ, regardless of their position within or "without" the "church". Paul explains further that "there is one body and one Spirit...one Lord, one faith, one baptism, one God and Father of all...but to each individual, Christ gave grace as He apportioned it" (Ephesians 4:4-7). And Christ distributed these roles to each member of his Body, whether they were part of an organized religious institution or not (Psalm 68:18).

The intention in giving each member of His Body one of these roles was to provide a vehicle by which the Body can mature and be unified. No man is an island. The Kingdom system was designed as a system of interdependence. Each person, in their individual role is called upon to function together with and in relationship with other members of the Body of Christ.

When I was first given the insight that the five-fold ministry was to be universally applied to the entire Body of Christ, whether they had active roles in the organized church or not, I received a lot of backlash against the idea. As usual, when confronted with an idea outside of normal church teachings, I sought answers in prayer. The response I got was threefold.

1. The Greek original text gives five categories with some: some as apostles, some prophets, etc. "There is no sixth category for those who do not belong to the others", The Lord told me.

2. "At the time that the five-fold was given to the Body as a gift, there was no organized structured religious institutional church. Church structure and organization came about hundreds of years later. How could those five roles have been designated solely for the church, if the 'church' hadn't been developed yet?"

3. "The five-fold was given as a gift to the Body to foster unity among the believers. The organized structured institutional church has held the five-fold captive since it was created. Has there been unity within the Body since then?"

There was no longer any question in my mind, after I received this answer. The five-fold was given by Christ as a gift to His Body to support and foster unity and maturity among the believers. This unity is to be unification under the headship and leadership of Christ. And unity within the Body would be proof that the five-fold was being correctly applied.

Through the implementation of the Kingdom design each member will attain maturity and recognize their position and function in the Body. This role is equally valid and vital to the Body, regardless of which sphere of influence it is practiced and fulfilled in. The role is also valid and vital to the Body as a whole, regardless of the religious denomination the member of the Body belongs to. The key to "living a life worthy of the calling that you have received"(Ephesians 4:1) is being in a relationship with God that is dependent and symbiotic.

People received the role that they were created to fulfill on this Earth when they were conceived (Psalm 139:13-18). This role remains hidden until it is sought out and uncovered. The process of uncovering one's purpose in life can be quick and easy or it can be long and painful. It can't, however, be avoided if the goal is to have any type of impact on this Earth while you are here. Once you discover your God-given role on Earth, the next step is to accept that role and function.

Accepting your place and purpose on Earth requires no small amount of humility: it requires accepting that we are not all equally endowed with every potential gift; and it requires accepting that others have gifts that we will never have, nor be able to imitate. Accepting your role on Earth also requires acknowledging the gift in other people without being envious of that gift. This is a process of maturation. The principle cornerstone of that maturation process is having developed a personal and dependent relationship with God. Developing that close relationship with a creator God will lead to greater trust, understanding, and acceptance of a divine order. When believers have accepted their place in that order and have acknowledged the wisdom of the plan, then they will "no longer be infants (in faith and understanding), tossed back and forth by the waves, and blown here and there by every wind of teaching and by the cunning and craftiness of people in their deceitful scheming" (Ephesians 4:14). Trends and fashions in the teaching of the Word will no longer have the ability to derail or detract members of the Body from their true destinies and callings. A member of the Body will have enough security and assurance in his or her calling to be able to stand against deceptions and manipulations.

The distribution of the roles to each member of His Body serves to support and develop the unity of the Body. This occurs by building up each member's dependence upon the head of the body, that is Christ himself. Christ gave the roles and functions to the entire Body of Christ in all of the spheres of influence or "mountains" as a gift, so that His Body would be built up. These functions equip each individual member of the Body, when accepted and implemented, for works of service within their calling (Ephesians 4:15-16). The roles and functions are dependent upon one another. No individual can reach his or her full potential without the support of the other four functions within that sphere of influence. It was designed as a system of interdependence. "Just as a body, though one, has many parts, but all its many part form one body, so it is with Christ" (1 Corinthians 12:12).

Christ is the head of His Body. The head leads the body. The body will go in the direction in which the head is facing. When an individual accepts Jesus as

Savior, he or she must accept that the position that they take up within His Body is not an independent one. The role and function of that individual within the Body was bought with a price (1 Corinthians 6:20; 7:23). Accepting that salvation is bought through the sacrifice of Jesus means that the person gives up fleshly "independence". In exchange for "independence" and the sin it causes, Godly "interdependence" under the leading and "headship" of Jesus needs to be accepted. His sheep follow His voice (John 10:27). We do not follow our own voice.

Additionally, the acceptance of the headship of Jesus should then lead to the acceptance of His design for His Body. His Body is not made up of one part, but of many (1 Corinthians 12:14). Each of these parts has a different job to do and different inherent skills, but each one is dependent upon the others to complete the task it was created for (1 Corinthians 12:4-6). Independence is not an option (1 Corinthians 12:15-17, 21-24). "God placed the parts in the body, every one of them, just as He wanted them to be" (1 Corinthians 12:18). Because God placed these parts in the Body Himself, His plan brings and will bring unity and harmony.

Jesus is truth and there is freedom in Him (2 Corinthians 3:17). This freedom is twofold. By accepting one's place within the Body structure you receive the freedom to be who God created you to be. You are a necessary and vital portion of the entire Body system. There is no one else who can do your job with exactly the same skill and proficiency that you can, because you were specifically created to fill that particular function. The second freedom in accepting the headship/Lordship of Jesus and accepting the Body structure is the freedom not to have to be someone who you were **not** created to be.

Many people spend their lives working in jobs and doing tasks that they were never meant for. The reasons for the misdirection can be many: misplaced loyalties, a sense of duty to family or others, etc. All of this disappears with the discovery of one's true identity. You were fearfully and wonderfully made and God knit you in your mother's womb (Psalm 139:14,19). You have a vital task to fulfill within the Body of Christ. Discovering who you are and what you were created to do is truth and that truth will set you free (John 8:32). If you would like to know who you are within the Body and what areas of society you were created to impact find out by visiting this page: **https://identitypassport.thrivecart.com/kingdom-come-passport/**

"Therefore, my brothers and sisters, make every effort to confirm your calling and election. For if you do these things, you will never stumble, and you will receive a rich welcome into the eternal kingdom of our Lord and Savior Jesus Christ." (II Peter 1:10-11) It is for this reason that it was written, "we see in part and we hear in part" (I Corinthians 13:11-12). The discovery of our God-given role and the placement within a unified grouping of the five ranks, called with a similar purpose, will provide the framework within which a believer will be able to function fully in his or her Kingdom calling.

RANK OF
REFORMER

The Reformer

The Reformers are sent to represent someone. Essentially, they function as diplomats, ambassadors, or emissaries. They carry the full authority of the one who sent them. This is the case regardless if a king, kingdom or another entity such as: a church, family, school, government organization, business, entertainment business, or media institution, sends them.

The term Reformer is also synonymous to the term apostle. Having its root in the Classic Greek terms: ἀπόστολος (*apóstolos*), meaning "one who is sent away", from στέλλω ("stello", "send") + ἀπό (*apo*, "away from"),[1] the literal translation into the English is "emissary", from the Latin *mitto* ("send") and *ex* ("from").[2] Another source of the term stems from military usage.

In Rome, during the 1st Century A.D., the term apostle was a commonly used military term. Applied to a certain breed of naval officer, it described a distinct type of individual. This person had a function similar to an admiral of a fleet of ships and was sent on special assignments to colonize new territories. They were ambassadors sent to represent the interests of Rome. In the days of colonization through Rome, apostles were called to go into new territories and to inform the inhabitants of that territory that they were now under a new governing authority. They brought with them the flag and the constitution of the new occupying government. Because they were emissaries, their job was to model and display the governing system and characteristics of the entity that they were sent to represent. In ancient Rome, they were walking, living, and breathing examples of Roman culture, civilization and the Roman way of life.

The Reformer is the first and highest rank; therefore, it encompasses the characteristics and aspects of all of the other four ranks. Because they are the frontrunners, during their assignments many Reformers also function as Revelators, Proclaimers, Nurturers and Educators. These parts of the assignment may be large portions of the overall mission, or they may play only a minor part. However, when taken together they represent the full picture of the ministry of Christ on Earth.

This means that Reformers working in a sphere of influence will sometimes take on the characteristics of the Revelators, Proclaimers, Nurturers and Educators depending upon what is needed at that particular place and time in order to fulfill their "mission". They will function within the talents and gifts that those ranks use as part of their efforts. These parts of the assignment may be large portions, or they may only consist of a minor part of the overall mission.

Because leadership and the unification of the ranks play an important role in Reformers' missions, they will often gravitate towards those positions in any organization. As such, Reformers in the mountain will always seek to work together with others to move a project forward. They are secure in their identities as Reformers. Therefore, they do not need to take credit for group efforts. They are content to work behind the scenes building others up and coordinating efforts to achieve the desired result.

Having the ability to operate using the talents of all of the other ranks, Reformers in a particular mountain will often have unusual insight into the workings of a certain aspect of the mountain or of the whole of the mountain. This places them in a unique position to be able to impact the workings of the mountain and to be able to impact others through projects, which come out of that mountain. They are dynamic people, and their words and actions will carry the power and authority of their rank.

Within the mountain, they have a strong drive to create order. They are the Reformers and with that rank comes all of the skills necessary to be able to reform things that are stuck or in need of reorganization. They will do this primarily by identifying people with a strong destiny in leadership and coming alongside them to mentor them and to help them mature. A Reformer has a built-in drive to change things or people. The sought after change has primarily to do with bringing a person, organization or project into alignment with the God-given destiny inherent to him, her, or it.

On some level, people might believe that the functions of the Reformer and the Nurturer are identical. However, where a Nurturer will seek to help a person or project into wholeness, the Reformer will seek to bring them into alignment with their God-ordained destiny. There should be no conflict between those two ranks. The two purposes and functions complement each other.

Reformers also carry an unusually strong gifting for entrepreneurship. They are the builders among the ranks. This building ability also manifests when assisting others in their efforts to construct new or innovative things. When placed in a situation, which draws on their constructive abilities, they will instinctively map out a plan to bring an idea into reality. You will often find them creating or financially supporting diverse activities. Those efforts will almost always yield financial gains, because the Reformer will draw on the gifts of the other ranks to examine the project from the vantage point of all the other ranks before moving forward on it.

They are the emissaries, among the ranks. They have a calling and were created for a specific time and purpose. When they recognize what that calling is, the potential to walk in the unusual will be released to assist them in that. They also have a strong code of ethics. As such, this will translate into creating an atmosphere in which people will cooperate and work together systematically to achieve that mountain's objectives.

There are levels of application of anything in life. Reformers can also operate in extremes. When they do, they can be perceived to be arrogant. They have an unusual gift of revelation. When that gift is not tempered and used in wisdom, Reformers can be seen as know-it-alls. Their strong code of ethics, actively pursued, can cause others to view them as dogmatic. Reformers have a built in drive to create order out of chaos. This can make them seem pushy, when this drive is exercised at an extreme. The Reformer is called to reform systems and people; taken to an extreme, others may view them as being intolerant of those that are reluctant to change.

Reformers are individuals that have a strong calling and destiny on their lives. That calling will draw them and send them into their particular sphere of influence to come beside other leaders to exhort and to lead with a view towards reformation. The change sought after by a Reformer is ultimately one, which will bring that system or that individual into alignment with the divine purpose for which it was created. Reformers lead, in order to lead back to God. If you think you are a Reformer, but aren't sure go here: **https://identitypassport.thrivecart.com/kingdom-come-passport/**

Characteristics of Reformers

- They work together with others
- They are dynamic and their words and actions carry power
- They have revelatory knowledge about and unusual insight into any sphere of influence or any task that they are given
- They create order
- They did not choose their assignment;
- their assignment chose them
- They walk in the unusual
- They have a strong code of ethics
- They work to build up those that are already in leadership positions as well as those that come after them
- They are entrepreneurs

RANK
OF
REVELATOR

The Revelator

Revelators are people of vision. They perceive things that might be and could be and set everything on sharing those visions from whichever platform they are given. They also see things clearly and with a heightened perception of right and wrong.

Revelators are also known as prophets. The word prophet comes from the Middle English: prophete; from the Old French: *prophete, profete*; from the Latin: prophēta and from the Greek: prophētēs/ προφήτης.

They are people who speak by divine inspiration or as an interpreter for divine revelation conveyed to them or through them. They are gifted with profound moral insight and exceptional powers of expression. In some cultures they are also known as soothsayers. Acting as predictors, they can sometimes end up being the chief spokespersons of a movement or cause.

True Revelators spend a lot of time thinking, meditating and practicing discernment before actually giving out a message or word. They understand the seriousness of their spoken word and have learned that not all things they see or hear are to be shared with others. This does not mean that the word will never be shared, they recognize that timing is a vital part of the revelations that they receive and that a right word at a wrong time can often produce more harm than good.

In addition, not everything they see will tickle the eyes and ears of others. They are committed to speaking the truth even if it is considered a "strong" or difficult word. Revelators are often the "whistleblowers" of society. They will not speak erroneously and declare something ok or acceptable in order to please the listener. They can often come across as overly dramatic to others in presenting their insights, when they use props to demonstrate their message.

Revelators are visionaries. They have special insight into the state of things and can quickly cut out all of the noise surrounding a situation to discern the heart of the matter and the facts associated with it. Then, everything is set on sharing those visions from whichever platform they are given. Because of this, they tend to gravitate towards occupations that allow them to utilize this talent.

Within the various mountains, a Revelator will seek out, or end up in jobs where they can use their unusual perception into trends and people. They will also help to reveal right or wrong in a situation or to help efforts, which are relevant and necessary to gain acceptance. Revelators have a source of insight that is greater than the normal intuition of the average person.

Their basis of inspiration and revelation is divine. New ideas, systems and developments take on an otherworldly quality when suggested by a Revelator. The Revelator will often hear "Nothing like that has ever been done before". They also have a knack for presenting exactly the right solution at the right time for whatever problem they are facing.

In the various mountains, this translates into a sixth-sense knowledge of what will be important, vital or influential, before anyone else recognizes it. This quality may cause a certain amount of jealousy in those that do not recognize or accept this Kingdom role. However, trend recognition is vital for the expansion of Kingdom on Earth. The ability to draw advancements from the spirit realm and to be able to verbalize these in such a way as to facilitate their translation into the natural realm is a key quality of this rank.

The Revelator is a speaker of the truth. In fact, upholding the truth is such an important ideal to this rank that this might end up rubbing people the wrong way. They are committed to speaking the truth even if it is considered to be "unpopular" or difficult. They are not interested in "towing the line" or being "yes-men" simply to please the listener. Because of this, they can come across as being overly dramatic, pushy, or loud.

When the quest for unbridled truth at all costs is not tempered with wisdom and grace, this characteristic of the rank can often lead to isolation. People seldom like to be confronted with their faults. In an organization or institution this is even more the case. This is why it is vitally important for a Revelator, perhaps even more so than the other ranks, to find a group of the other four ranks in which they can integrate. Since they already have a tendency toward being isolated, their collaboration with the other four ranks will offer them a troop to belong to and accountability as well.

Their love of the truth even includes being realistic about their own shortcomings. The self-examination necessary to come to terms with one's failures protects this rank from pride, which may come from the fact that they have insights that other ranks lack. True humility is a hallmark of someone walking in the strength of this position in the Kingdom.

The Revelator plays a vital role in bringing insight into trends and streams. When they have found a cause to commit themselves to, they are a key player in the team of five ranks. They offer unusual revelation and insight as to the true status of any situation or problem facing the group. They are the ones with an answer and a strategy, when it looks like none is available.

There has been some confusion in determining the difference between the rank of Revelator and the gift of the prophetic, which all believers in Christ have access to. The rank of Revelator carries with it the authority to admonish in addition to the obligation of encouraging. They cut through deception and uncover truth, exposing flaws that need to be addressed and bringing unusual and innovative solutions to the table. In many cases, this may cause them to become unpopular, which could lead to isolation and a feeling of loneliness.

Within any context, however, even those outside of the institutional church, the ability to discern and uncover facts can provide an advantage to an organization or institution that uses it. The truth, used wisely and in a timely fashion, will provide that entity with a leg up over the competition. Given this, why would anyone want to avoid the truth and shun the gift of a Revelator? They are an important part of any "fab-five" team.

When operating in the extreme, a Revelator can be perceived as being mean-spirited, because of their need to pronounce the truth at all costs. It is for this same reason that others may consider them to be extremely judgmental. They have a strong drive to express the visions and innovations that they perceive, which can lead to them being labeled by others as Drama Queens. Their heightened insights, when left un-tempered by wisdom, will cause them to earn the title of know-it-all. Ultimately, walking in this rank without a measure of maturity, will lead to isolation. Are you a Revelator? Go here to find out:
https://identitypassport.thrivecart.com/kingdom-come-passport/

Characteristics of Revelators

- They feel compelled to verbally express their thoughts and ideas
- They believe in calling out criminal and/or immoral behavior
- They have an enhanced sensitivity for the truth
- They are great believers in justice
- They are eager and willing to embrace suffering or stand alone to maintain the integrity of their message
- They often manifest insight, foresight, or oversight
- They are open and honest about their own failures and faults
- They can become non-relational, due to their whistleblower role
- They will commit themselves wholeheartedly to a cause they believe in

RANK OF
PROCLAIMER

The Proclaimer

The Proclaimer has a vital role in society. Proclaimers are the ones who convince. Their life's calling is to convince people to use the things and adopt the ideas that they are most passionate about. Proclaimers BELIEVE and because they believe, they feel called to persuade others to believe in the same things that they do. The success or failure of an undertaking pursued by a Proclaimer rests entirely upon the number of converts to their cause and the level of enthusiasm exhibited by those converts.

The term Proclaimer is also synonymous with the word evangelist. Having its root in the Late Latin term *evangelista*. It also stems from the Ancient Greek term *euangelistes*/ εὐαγγελιστής "preacher of the gospel," literally "bringer of good news". Additionally, the term evangelist can trace its roots from the Greek *euangelizesthai*/ εὐαγγελίζεσθαι "to evangelize" from *euángelos*/ εὐάγγελος "bringing good news", from *eu-* εὖ "good" + ἀγγέλλειν *angellein* "announce," and from *angelos* "messenger".

Taken together, this means that a Proclaimer/evangelist is a bringer of good news – a messenger. They carry information with a view towards spreading the content by convincing others to carry it with a similarity of passion. Proclaimers are the "marketers" and "salespeople" in the divine social order. They are the convincers and influencers. They move and work in different areas of society and can easily be spotted through their high levels of enthusiasm for their message. They are not just found in one sphere of society, instead, they can be found in virtually every business and organization.

There are two major types of Proclaimer in the world. The first is the "Lone Ranger" Proclaimer. This is a person who travels the world, or their sphere of influence, drumming up support for their pet cause. They tend to work alone and move wherever they are led to find the next audience for their "message". Because of this, their message tends to be perceived as a personal message. The messenger then becomes the author of the message, whether or not that is the case. It is imperative for the "Lone Ranger" Proclaimer to have a group to whom they are accountable.

The second type of Proclaimer congregates in groups. Within the group, the

Proclaimer will find a "team" to carefully craft the message in a form most appealing to a mass audience. They will draw from the strengths of others to support a common cause. This type of Proclaimer understands that there is safety in numbers. Having become part of a team, this type of Proclaimer will draw the necessary strength off of this relationship in order to carry the message to a wider audience. Being accountable to a team will insure that both the messenger and the message retain their authenticity.

"Lone Ranger" or group, it is extremely important that both types of Proclaimer be associated with the other ranks in some form or another. Within a "fab-five" grouping, the giftings of the other ranks will support and augment the role of the Proclaimer and the integrity of the message will be supported and maintained.

Proclaimers are the sellers, the ones who exist to persuade people to use the things and adopt ideas. When they move in this capacity, they can be almost mesmerizing in their ability to do just that. They are at their most compelling, when they truly believe and stand behind what they are selling.

When Proclaimers BELIEVE, because they believe, they feel called to persuade others to be certain of the same things that they are certain of. They are passionate about what they are "selling". When they are operating out of a positive motivation, they will attempt to convince others out of compassion. They will persuade, because they are convinced that the adoption of their viewpoint will be for the benefit of the recipient.

This means that within the mountains Proclaimers believe that they are called to present information in the most compelling way possible. They love the place and the task that they are called to work at. As a result, they have urgency about their message and are bold and intentional about the pursuit of converts.

Proclaimers will have unusual wisdom about how to most effectively spread the message that they want to get out. They are intelligent and they have a high level of knowledge about their subject and field of expertise. Often, it is through their understanding of the subject that they are able to present the information in such a way as to sway opinions.

This skill, as well as their unusual charisma and other talents make Proclaimers consummate communicators. As such, they have all of the skills and talents necessary to be able to influence large audiences through media of any type. Marketing and advertising departments are often staffed with a large number of Proclaimers.

Because their calling is to influence people to adopt a specific viewpoint, Proclaimers can potentially operate out of a weakness. This lies in the fact that their perception of a job well done is often colored by results, which cannot be completely controlled or influenced. Operating out of weakness, that is, being driven to "sell" more, and reach more, this rank can potentially use unfair tactics, or manipulation, to reach its goals. The success or failure of an undertaking pursued by a Proclaimer could then potentially rest entirely upon the number of converts to their cause and the level of enthusiasm exhibited by those converts. This could then lead to a concentration on gathering numbers as proof. Focusing on an increase in numbers, come what may, ultimately leads to a breakdown in character and values.

However, when operating out of right motivations, the Proclaimer will concentrate on viewing success in terms of the manifestation of changes brought about as a result of the encounter with the message. It is for this reason that it is imperative for this rank to belong to a group consisting of the other ranks, which are all pursuing the same objective. This integration into a collective will offer accountability to the Proclaimer and bring balance to their message.

When operating in the extreme, Proclaimers may be seen as being overpowering, because their enthusiasm for their message will cause them to interrupt others. For the same reason they may also be considered loud and opinionated. Walking in the weakness of this rank may cause Proclaimers to become pushy, in a drive to achieve more and "sell" more. Ultimately, this ambitious energy may even lead them to be willing to compromise integrity and use outrageous tactics or manipulation to achieve their goals. Do you think you are a Proclaimer? Go here to find out for sure:
https://identitypassport.thrivecart.com/kingdom-come-passport/

Characteristics of Proclaimers

- They are bold and intentional in their pursuit of converts
- They persuade, because they believe that their viewpoint will benefit others
- They have great skill in influencing others when they use a perceived course of actions
- Their knowledge of a subject is often the avenue used to sway opinions
- They see their efforts as fulfillment in their lives
- They lead others to believe in their passions, by kindling fires and inspiring
- They feel an urgency to push to bring others along their path
- They are consummate communicators and can adjust to suit an audience
- They sometimes have unusual gifts and charisma that help them to sway a group

RANK OF
NURTURER

The Nurturer

Nurturers are called to protect and develop a group of people or whole organizations. They are adept at working with people. The term Nurturer is also synonymous with the word shepherd. The term shepherd stems from the Old English *sceaphierde* (*scēaphierde*), a compound of *scēap* ("sheep") and *hierde* ("herdsman"). The origin for the word shepherd (pastor) in the Old English stems from three key Greek words. They are (1) poimen/ ποιμήν, (2) presbuteros/ πρεσβύτερος, and (3) episkopos/ ἐπίσκοπος. They are consecutively translated as (1) shepherd or pastor, (2) elder, and (3) overseer or bishop. In the English, the verb shepherd means to guide or guard someone or something in the manner of a shepherd.

A 5000-year-old tradition, the herding of sheep is one of the oldest occupations. Sheep were, and still are, valuable. As a commodity that produces milk, meat and wool, they are a significant economic factor. Therefore, the care and the nurturing of this livestock play an important part in agricultural economics. Historically, it is the youngest child in an agricultural family that got the job of tending to the safety and welfare of the sheep.

A very limber form of livestock, sheep can climb to higher altitudes and can feed in rough terrain that is wholly unsuitable for cattle or other domesticated animals. A shepherd is therefore, of necessity, a person who is limber and able to climb into places where the sheep feed. They carry a strong multi-purpose stick in the form of a hook that can be used for balance, examining dangerous undergrowth and for defense against attacking predators. The use of the hook/crook allows for the recovery of fallen animals by ensnaring them by the neck or leg. Synonyms to the term shepherd include: coach, counsel, lead, mentor, pilot, guide, show, and tutor. When compiling the definitions given above, the term "shepherd", which we have called Nurturer, denotes a person, who is called to a position of oversight over others. They are limber and adept at finding the "lost" and returning those to a position within a group. They are fearless in their defense of their "charges" and will sacrifice in order to achieve the highest good for that individual or for an organization that they are in charge of.

Nurturers are called to protect and develop individuals, groups of people, whole organizations, or even systems or specific things. They have a talent for recognizing the intrinsic value of someone or something and then approaching that person or entity in such a way as to draw the best out of them or it. Within the various mountains, Nurturers are the ones who "take care of" people or things. They are the personal assistants, the talent agents as well as coaches and scouts.

Nurturers also "take care" of groups of people or things. They seek their good in every decision they make and seek always to protect their "charges" from that which could harm them both from within and without. Called to the various mountains, the Nurturer will gravitate towards a position which puts them "in charge" of the well being of someone or something. Once put in this type of a position, they will grow into their role of protector and cultivator.

It is the Nurturer who is called to see the potential in something or someone and to invest the time and effort necessary to draw that potential out. Often, this talent is called for when the person or thing is too "far gone" for others to deal with. It is in this situation, that the Nurturer will blossom to his/her greatest potential. They are capable of taking the worst case, the one no one else wants to invest in, and slowly coax the potential out of the person or situation. They are the "firemen" in the world. They run into burning buildings and save people.

The Nurturer, ultimately, is called to husband others. Those "others" can include human beings, animals, objects, organizations or institutions. The idea of husbandry is to seek the highest good for the person, place or thing being "husbanded". Within that context, the Nurturer will assist that person, place or thing to achieve integrity of self and wholeness. The process of achieving wholeness may be uncomfortable and, in certain instances, painful. But, that process, as long as the object of "husbandry" is willing, will ultimately lead to the wholeness of the subject.

Nurturers are limber and adept at finding the "lost" and returning those to a position within a group. They will go to great lengths to look for those that have been rejected and marginalized. When they find those that are lost, they will expend great amounts of energy and effort in order to bring those "lost sheep" into wholeness and right relationship to the rest of the group. They are fearless in their defense of their "charges" and will sacrifice in order to achieve the highest good for that individual, that place, or for an organization that they are in charge of.

They thrive in places where they can work with others to create safe environments. These settings will be points where people, or things, or systems are given the support and cultivation necessary to reach their greatest potential. This is achieved by bringing them to wholeness. The wholeness is to be brought about both on the individual as well as corporate level

Operating out of a desire for the greater good of everyone involved, they will, depending upon the mountain to which they are called, even draw a circle around those they are nurturing, which can include an entire town, region, nation, or the planet itself. There is no limit to the capacity of a Nurturer to nurture. There is no limit to the scale of assignment that a Nurturer can be called to.

Having found a position within organizations that allows them to operate in their function and utilize all of their talents, the Nurturer is a loyal member of the team. Their keen insight into the needs of team members and of the systems included in projects, lend support to the entire fabric of the undertaking. Nurturers have the task of supporting growth and development by promoting health and wholeness to individuals, groups, places and things.

When functioning in the extreme, Nurturers may seem to be controlling. Their drive to provide safety for their charges may also leave the impression of being over-protecting. Nurturers work closely with those that are assisting. In some cases this may be viewed as an attempt at creating co-dependency. Their tendency to help, protect and guide may also, when taken to an extreme, be seen as an attempt to discourage creativity and curiosity in others. They invest great amounts of love in their work. This may lead to them becoming oversensitive and making it "all be about them". Are you convinced that you are a Nurturer? Go here to find out for sure: **https://identitypassport.thrivecart.com/kingdom-come-passport/**

Characteristics of Nurturers

- They are adept at finding the issues that need to be addressed
- They are more apt than other ranks at seeing the good in everyone
- Disciplining and correcting belong to their responsibilities
- They are protective of their charges
- They help others find their passion and develop their talents
- They are gifted at creating harmony or unity within groups
- They extend love as they care for those that they keep
- They work through example to transform dysfunctional people/ organizations into the functional
- They are self-controlled, sensible and respectful of everyone.

RANK OF
EDUCATOR

The Educator

Educators are the informers in society. They are people who spread knowledge and insights to others. Working in the highest level of their function, they research and then pass acquired understanding to others. They do this with a view towards the betterment of the individual, group, organization or even the planet as a whole.

The term Educator is synonymous with the word teacher. The Latin word for teacher is **doctor.** In Greek, the term is didaskalon or διδάσκαλον. The Greek definition of the term includes a widening of the classic perception. In addition to teaching, the educator also has the duty to direct the course of action and to admonish.

Educators have a thirst for knowledge and can spend many hours reading, researching, and developing a clear course of instruction. When left untempered, this may lead to a life of seclusion as they develop their thoughts and insights and lose track of everything else around them. For this reason, it is imperative for an Educator to be integrated into a group including the other ranks.

Their greatest passion is to impart knowledge so that others might grow. This process of facilitating the digestion of knowledge requires more than just studying the subject and dumping that information on a recipient. In addition to the skill of teaching, the best Educators will also be consummate social workers and managers. They are able to manage the pace and flow of information in the environment in which the material is taught and they are able to recognize the personal situations of the subjects which might hinder the absorption of and the adaptation of the material.

The very best Educators will often have, and display these personal attributes:

1. They are passionate about what they are teaching;
2. They are willing to learn as they know they need to stay on top of their subject;
3. Their subject matter and the way in which they present their subject matter is inspirational;

4. They have empathy with their students;
5. They have a positive mental attitude;
6. They are open to change;
7. They are a role model for their students;
8. They are creative;
9. They have a sense of humor;
10. They have honed their presentation skills;
11. They maintain a sense of calmness regardless of the situation in which they find themselves;
12. They are respectful toward their listeners.

Educators play a vital role in the mountains. Because they are people who pass knowledge and acquired understanding on to others, they realize that there is a price to be paid for gaining knowledge and they are willing to pay it. They are excellent trainers and researchers.

They are the ones that delve deeply into a particular topic searching out information from a variety of sources and then cross-referencing those sources to uncover the truth. True Educators value truth as the highest possible good. They have a low tolerance for distortions of the truth and manipulations of the truth to serve ulterior motives.

When they are researching topics, they will often receive a special understanding of the topic that isn't readily available to others. Because of this, they often have insight which, when presented, enables others to easily grasp the concept. They are excellent instructors. Within the mountains, these gifts lend themselves to tasks or positions calling for focus and intensity.

As driven as Educators can be in the quest for understanding, they can be equally enamored with the process of interacting with those who are acquiring that knowledge from them. To an Educator, understanding is not simply something to be passed from one person to another or from one person to a group of people. Instead, they believe that interaction with students will lead to a greater revelation of the topic at hand.

This drive may cause educators to push for more interactive options for their charges and ultimately cause the creation of new technologies, which allow constant interaction between the presenter and the audience. Educators recognize that current advances in technology provide increasing opportunities to reach wider audiences with information. These include innovations in teaching techniques as well as teaching methodologies.

The ultimate purpose for imparting knowledge is not just growing understanding, the most effective Educators believe. Instead, instruction should yield changes in behavioral patterns as well. The best Educators are also called to admonish those they are instructing, when their choices are not in their own best interest. The instruction imparted should be transformational, yielding measurable differences in attitudes and in the quality of life of the ones being taught.

This means that an Educator within the mountains is called to influence others. This influence is not simply an exercise in spreading information on multiple levels or scales. In the highest sense of the calling, an Educator will align him/herself with projects that produce life-transforming messages through the spread of information as well as the communication of educational material designed to cause transformation through deep reflection.

Within the context of a group including the other four ranks, the Educator will be the member of the group in charge of making sure that all of the other members have the most up-to-date and relevant information necessary to support the common project. This function will include doing the research and then finding the most effective method for sharing that data with the rest of the group. As the project or initiative advances, so will the data and the Educator will make sure that any additional information reaches the group as they need it. The Educator serves the group, by making sure all pertinent information is available in real time.

When operating in extremes, Educators can sometimes be perceived as being stern. Their thirst for insight can leave the impression that they are driven and boring. Having acquired the sought after understanding, their great enthusiasm for sharing this knowledge may lead to others seeing them as being know-it-alls. Educators are truth seekers. Once having found the truth and having made up their mind about that particular topic, the knowledge must be tempered with wisdom. If this knowledge is not tempered with wisdom, the sharing of that "truth" can leave the impression that the Educator

is intolerant of others viewpoints. Want to find out if you are an Educator?
Go here to check:
https://identitypassport.thrivecart.com/kingdom-come-passport/

Characteristics of Educators

- They use all of their skills to research subjects of interest
- They use divine inspiration and analysis to find deeper understanding
- They love to talk and share their findings with others and also publish them
- They have strong presentation skills using various methods to increase knowledge
- They provoke curiosity to bring greater revelation of the topic
- They use instruction to drive changes in behavioral patterns
- They admonish, when choices are not in the best interest of their students
- They are called to expand comprehension
- They are able to transfer their passion for learning and becoming the best to others

We're All in This Together

Every human being on the planet was created by God to carry a singular destiny and to fulfill a unique function. In order to establish order, God gave every individual specific and unique characteristics that are designed to help that person fill a specific role. There are five of these roles. These characteristics and these roles are not exclusive to Christians, because God created everyone equally and it is His desire that "ALL should be saved and come to the knowledge of the truth" (1 Timothy 2:4). The person is then given a choice as to whether they use that role to advance light or to advance darkness.

I have tried, to the best of my ability, to describe the characteristics, functions, and roles in God's order the way it was explained to me in prayer. If there is any confusion about these roles the problem doesn't lie in the design but certainly in the messenger.

If there is any doubt as to the universal nature of these roles, I would challenge anyone reading this to begin to look at the people in your life, or those visible to the public, and try to figure out which one of these roles these people fulfill. You will be surprised. Rebecca Rhodes and I often use movies as a way to test the universality of God's Kingdom structure. If these ranks are distributed to everyone, everywhere then they should be visible in everyone, everywhere.

In a nutshell you can usually tell who is a Reformer by the wake of change that they leave behind them. Change is part of their DNA. They can't help it. If they enter a room things begin to shift and morph around them. A Revelator is always in the know long before anyone else gets it. A Proclaimer, generally speaking, is the loudest, most convincing person in a group. And they are relentless. Once they have been convinced of something they will continue to hammer that point home until everyone else around them believes the same thing. The Nurturer is usually the person in a crowd that everyone dumps their "stuff" onto. They are the ones people go to with their problems. They are the ones in families that try to fix everyone else's problems. Usually that involves helping the person to grow, mature, and become whole. Finally the Educator is the person in a group that always has the answers to questions or knows exactly where to go to get those answers.

They gather and disseminate information wherever it is needed.

It might be difficult to pinpoint a person's or movie character's rank. On the whole, however, after careful observation, that position ultimately becomes clear. The order and structure of the divine design will eventually become visible and obvious regardless if the context is spiritual, religious, or not. It really has become apparent to me that God has, indeed, created a universal order that applies to all of society. He really has knit each one of us in our mother's womb and He really does want every human being on the planet to be saved and come to the knowledge of the truth. This chapter examined the first aspect of God's Kingdom Structure, the ranks. How those ranks interact with one another and how they ultimately build a cohesive team will be discussed further in Chapter Seven.

---

[1] Liddell & Scott's Greek-English Lexicon, Oxford, 1944

[2] Cassell's Latin Dictionary, Revised by Marchant & Charles

The

Mountains

Chapter Six – The Mountains

The Mountains and Their Order

The original message given to Bill Bright, Loren Cunningham and Francis Schaefer was the schematic plan (to use an architectural term) to transform society. Anyone who is familiar with building or architecture recognizes that a schematic plan is a rough draft of something. It will give you the general idea of what is going to be built, but it can never give you every detail. Those details come as the plan is discussed with the client and specific wishes are built into the design. The schematic plan then becomes a final plan.

There have been a number of "client meetings" since the original schematic design was given to the Body of Christ. One of them came about when Mark Chironna and Lance Wallnau had a telephone conversation, which led to the mandate being renamed the "Seven Mountain" message. Although both men were seemingly unaware of it at the time, they were holding a "client meeting" with the Holy Spirit, and the Spirit adjusted the plan at that meeting.

I would imagine, that there have been many other attempts by God to add details to the schematic since then. I know of a few books written by Johnny Enlow on the topic. I am also aware of a book, written by Lance Wallnau and Bill Johnson, that discusses aspects of the mountain message. Apparently, there seems to have been some difficulty in the mainstream church grasping the client's wishes and transferring that to the plan. Why otherwise would God have picked an architect and city planner, who was not a full-time minister, nor had she traveled the "traditional" path of ministry, to translate His wishes into a final plan? Believe me, I am still trying to wrap my head around that one myself.

Over the span of two years, God held some pretty intense "client meetings" with me. I "get" architecture; I also understand quite a few things about sociology and how to apply that into city planning projects. The problem I had was when God started downloading and explaining the "Church" aspect of His design to me. It was so foreign to me that it was like giving a fish a bicycle to ride (to hijack a German expression). All I could do was to stop the flow of information and ask for clarification before I crashed the bike or a tire fell off. God was very patient with me. He always made sure to explain things in terms that I could understand.

In addition to the explanations of the ranks and their function in the Kingdom, another major design change came as a result of those "client meetings". During those "meetings", an eighth mountain was revealed. This does not, in any way, shape, or form, detract from the original message that there are seven mountains, or spheres of influence, which are critically important in the effort to disciple nations for Christ. Instead it supports it and adds to it, as the additional mountain can easily be found in numerous scriptural texts.

The eighth mountain is the Kingdom Mountain and its primary function is a coordinating one. It is the level of command above the other mountains and its purpose it to connect people and efforts in the other mountains together. It is administrative and organizational in nature. The people called to this mountain will work together with, or in, one or many different mountains in order to support Kingdom advancements and efforts.

An additional design adjustment that happened in those meetings was the inclusion of a specific order or hierarchy to the mountains. What I was shown is that there will be efforts to advance the teachings of Jesus and the values of the Judeo-Christian-tradition taking place in all of the mountains simultaneously. In order to cause those efforts to trigger an avalanche or to set a chain of dominos in motion, it is necessary to focus on the first of those mountains. This is because the values of a society are anchored in the Church Mountain. The Church Mountain is the first of the seven spheres of societal influence.

When the values of a society are settled and a certain level of understanding about the purpose of that first mountain has been achieved. An implementation of that purpose will follow. When those two steps are taken, a tipping point will have been reached. The efforts that follow in the next mountains will have more power and impact. Then, like a chain of dominos, the mountains will turn to Jesus and their effort, energy and enthusiasm will spill into the next mountain catapulting that mountain further than it could have achieved on its own.

At this point, it would probably be confusing to get into a discussion of the different mountains and how they interact with one another. Suffice it to say that there is an order and hierarchy to the different spheres of influence in society. Each one has a specific role to play in the Kingdom structure, and each mountain interacts with the others in a specific way. A discussion of those aspects of the Kingdom plan will take place in Chapter Seven, after a general understanding of the individual mountains and their purposes has been reached.

The information that follows has been grouped into the different mountains. These have been placed in order from the top mountain to the bottom mountain. Within each of the descriptions of the various mountains, verses of the Bible are given that offer more insight into the various aspects of each mountain. An etymology of the terms offers an additional layer to understanding. Finally, information about the roles of individuals called to the sphere of influence has been included, so that readers can begin to understand their position within the Kingdom structure, when they have discovered it.

The social problems that we are confronted with every time we turn on the news or open a newspaper are a direct reflection of the confusion in the Body of Christ as to its role in society. For generations the Church was told it only had a supporting role to play in society. The Body of Christ was herded into a continual state of passivity in a pasture of perpetual waiting. The Body was waiting for rapture, waiting for an exit from this evil world, and pointing the figure at others for not taking responsibility for the state of things. Instead of taking ownership of the situation and stepping out in its God-given authority, it blamed others. It blindly followed the lead of the pastor instead of the leadings of The Holy Spirit.

A new day is dawning. Believers are waking up to their responsibilities. The Covid 19 pandemic, which shut down so many churches for such a long period of time, caused many believers to re-examine their relationship with their churches. It also re-ignited many believers' direct relationships with their God. Finding their position in God's design is the next step in bringing His Kingdom on Earth.

KINGDOM
MOUNTAIN

The Kingdom Mountain

Micah 4:1 - NLT
*In the last days, the mountain of the LORD's house will be the highest of all--
the most important place on earth. It will be raised above the other hills, and
people from all over the world will stream there to worship.*

Isaiah 2:2 - NIV
*In the last days the mountain of the LORD's temple will be established as the
highest of the mountains; it will be exalted above the hills, and all nations
will stream to it.*

Daniel 7:18 - NIV
*But the holy people of the Most High will receive the kingdom and will
possess it forever--yes, forever and ever.*

The word kingdom comes from the Greek language. Monarchies in ancient
Greece could have two forms, which resulted in the development of two
words that can be translated into the English word kingdom: a good one,
basileia (βασιλεία); and a bad one, tyrannis (τύραννος). "The main criterion
for basileia, to be translated here as "royalty" or "kingship", was to rule
according to the law and for the benefit of the subjects." Wilson, Nigel,
Encyclopedia of Ancient Greece, pg. 480.

Many in the Body of Christ believe that God's Kingdom will manifest as a
result of a Rapture and sovereign establishment of Jesus' reign through His
return. As convenient as this viewpoint is, it is difficult to find the scriptural
basis for this conviction. Instead, there are endless scriptural texts and
Biblical accounts that establish the reality of a partnership between mankind
and God: Genesis 1:26, 28, 18:16-33, Exodus 32:12-14, Judges 7, Matthew
25:21, Galatians 3:29, 4:7, Ephesians 3:6, Colossians 1:24, 2 Timothy 2:12, 1
Peter 4:13, Revelation 21:7.

When Jesus taught His disciples to pray in Matthew 6:10, He admonished
them to pray to God that *"your Kingdom come...on Earth as it is in Heaven"*.
Jesus also taught them, in that verse, **how** God's Kingdom was to manifest on
Earth: *"your Will be done on Earth as it is in Heaven"*. So, even minimally,
believers are called to pray that His Kingdom be brought and implemented on

Earth. Additionally, the previously mentioned verses of Isaiah 2:2 and Micah 4:1 both state that the mountain (read: God's government) of the Lord's temple would be established as the highest of all of the mountains **in the last days** and that it would be exalted in all of the hills (read: man's governmental and organizational structures) and all nations would be drawn to it.

The Kingdom (basileia) will come on Earth, when the church (ekklesia) begins to corporately submit to the Will of God in every aspect of their lives. "The church is constituted by those who are entering and receiving the reign of God. It is where the children of the reign corporately manifest the presence and characteristic features of God's reign. The divine reign expresses itself in a unique, though not exhaustive or exclusive, fashion in the church." Hunsberger, George R., The Story that Chooses Us, Kindle version.

The scripture is clear, that *"those who are led by the Spirit of God are the children of God"* Romans 8:14. The children of God are the members of the ekklesia who have submitted themselves to the leadings of the Holy Spirit. Romans 8:16. This is a clear prerequisite to being able to be used by The Spirit to manifest the Kingdom of God on Earth, as it is not possible for a person with divided loyalties to step into that authority. *"What agreement is there between the temple of God and idols? For we are the temple of the living God. As God has said: 'I will live with them and walk among them, and I will be their God, and they will be my people.'"* 2 Corinthians 6:16.

In Daniel 22:45, Daniel is describing the faithful followers and doers of the word of Jesus when he explained the concept of a rock, which grew to become a mountain and overtook the hills of the world. Daniel is describing an End Times move of God through the faithful disciples and servants of Christ, which will expand and grow to encompass the entire Earth and swallow all of the established human structures and organizations, including the political structures established by men. This concept can be found in many other Biblical texts, one of which is the much cited verse of Isaiah 11:9, *"...They shall not hurt nor destroy in all My Holy Mountain: for the Earth shall be full of the knowledge of the Lord, as the waters cover the sea."*

The Kingdom of God will manifest on Earth when the believing sons and daughters of God submit their lives and everything that they do to the leadings of The Holy Spirit. In this way, these people will be able to move into every sphere of influence, or "mountain" of government in society and will begin to affect these areas. From the Kingdom level of influence, this will be done by coming alongside initiatives in the other mountains and assisting them in their efforts. It will also be accomplished by creating initiatives, which connect smaller efforts in various mountains together. The Kingdom Mountain operates from a higher perspective. In order to implement the overall objective, it serves to give direction, guidance and encourage initiatives from that vantage point. It is the command center for the battle to influence culture. People working out of the Kingdom Mountain have a special authority to be able to influence and cause major shifts of cultures and values.

When they are moving in their calling, people in the Kingdom Mountain will use their sphere of influence to affect operations in one of the mountains, a number of mountains simultaneously, or a number of mountains successively. They are not bound to the constraints of any particular mountain, but have the freedom to move between the mountains and connect, support or create initiatives whenever they are led to do so. Depending upon their rank, their impact on the initiatives meant to bring the Kingdom to Earth will differ. The goal of all of their efforts will be to spread knowledge about Kingdom initiatives and efforts from one arena to another and ultimately to connect various efforts together whenever it is called for. The bringing of the Kingdom on Earth is their objective.

Often, initiatives founded by Kingdom Mountain people will offer the opportunity for people of various mountains to work together to implement the objectives. People called to the Kingdom Mountain are the moderators and mediators of the Kingdom. They live under the understanding that combined strength yields unilateral victories, whereas singular strength is limited in the transformational effect it can achieve.

Working out of the Kingdom Mountain requires an enormous level of humility. Because the purpose of the mountain is to be the command central and coordinating base for the implementation of the Kingdom in all mountains and spheres of influence, people with a calling to the Kingdom Mountain are constantly required to push their personal wishes and desires to the background. When called to come alongside an initiative in one of the other mountains, that initiative will have the priority and they will assist with every talent and ability that they possess. People called to the Kingdom Mountain are true servants. They have a servant's heart and live to promote the activities of the other mountains and of the Kingdom. They will give up their own agendas in an effort to support the greater good of the whole structure.

Characteristics of The Kingdom Mountain

- It influences all spheres of society
- It is non-denominational, inter-generational and is not ethnocentric
- It serves all other mountains or spheres of influence
- It provides the organizational structure for impacting the fabric of the entire society
- It serves the initiatives in the other mountains.
- Based upon Godly values, principles, and behaviors, it moves out to bring worldly systems into alignment with those values and behaviors
- Its purpose is to connect initiatives in various mountains to apply the foundational principles
- It holds integrity and the application of that message in every arena of society to be of the highest importance
- In its highest form, it draws the true, noble, right, pure, lovely, admirable, excellent or praiseworthy characteristics (Philippians 4:8) out of people.
- Its foundational values will serve to bring the highest level of quality of life and prosperity
- People working out of the mountain have a special authority to be able to cause major shifts of cultures and values

CHURCH MOUNTAIN

The Church Mountain

Acts 20:28 - NIV
Keep watch over yourselves and all the flock of which the Holy Spirit has made you overseers. Be shepherds of the church of God, which he bought with his own blood.

Romans 10:15 – Jubilee Bible 2000
And how shall they preach if they have not been sent? As it is written, How beautiful are the feet of those that announce the gospel of peace, of those that announce the gospel of that which is good!

The origin of the word "church" stems from Middle English *chirche*, from Old English *ċiriċe* ("church"), from Proto-Germanic *kirikǭ*, an early borrowing of Ancient Greek κυριακόν (*kuriakón*), neuter form of κυριακός (*kuriakós*, "belonging to the lord"), from κύριος (*kúrios*, "ruler, lord"), from Proto-Indo-European **ḱēw-*, **ḱwā-* ("to swell, spread out, be strong, prevail"). Another stem comes from the Greek word ἐκκλησία, ας, ἡ (ekklésia: an assembly, a (religious) congregation). Ekklésia stems from the roots ek ("out from and to") and kaléō ("to call"). So where the Greek term *kirikǭ* ultimately produced the word "church", the other Greek term ekklésia produced the words ecclesiology and ecclesiastical, both strongly associated with the Church or churches in general.

Taken together, therefore, the church is an assembly or a congregation of individuals modeling a set of values. First and foremost, it is called to "come out" of the world. This requires a separation from the world's way of doing things and a consecration and dedication to higher purposes. It is then called to swell, spread out, be strong, prevail, and to go out into the world. The church has a function, and that is to be the source of a group's or nation's values, behaviors, language, and rituals. It establishes the model of appropriate behavior for the culture in which it is found.

Every society and every sphere of influence is affected by the standard set up in the church. Therefore, the standard upheld by that entity must be one based upon an unshakeable set of moral and ethical standards. These standards are then implemented in succession in each of the subsequent areas of influence. Once spread throughout society, they permeate and affect every single aspect of life within that culture. Because the church is the source of societal values, behaviors, language and rituals, a policy of strict adherence to those established set of values must be implemented and maintained. A disconnect between the principals touted by the leadership and those actually practiced by them will ultimately cause a total rejection of those values on every level. The church must practice what it preaches.

There has been a gradual erosion of the values that shaped Western civilization through the advent and advancement of the idea of secular humanism. The foundational Judeo-Christian values have been systematically attacked and eroded by special interest groups trying to undermine the very fabric of society. The root cause of the erosion of the values, however, is not the advancement of the other value systems, but the relinquishing of territory formerly held by the Church. This has occurred primarily through passivity. The church has voluntarily given up the ground that it once held and dominated.

The Church Mountain (or Mountain of Religion) offers the dominant determining system of values, morals and beliefs implemented in a nation, society or group. The question constantly being posed within the Western society has been if Christianity offers the best option. Buddhism, Hindi, Atheism, Islam, Secular Humanism and many others have tried to take the place of the Judeo-Christian tradition in the West, claiming that they are the better alternative to an aging and outdated social value system. The lack of resistance by The Church has allowed that to happen. Ironically, the Church in the West has been losing ground to Secular Humanism at the same time other former Communist nations have been allowing the Judeo-Christian values to take hold and expand in their nations. The government of China, for example, has recognized the connection between the growth, wealth and influence of nations and the Christian values of those nations.[1]

While historic works, such as Max Weber's, *The Protestant Ethic and the Spirit of Capitalism*[2] have given scientific basis to the claim of the superiority of the Christian value system, newer works also examine this thesis. In Vishal Mangalwadi's book, *The Book that Made Your World: How the Bible Created the Soul of Western Civilization*[3], the author examines all of the major world religions and compares their value systems to one another and reaches the conclusion that the Judeo-Christian tradition of the West produces the highest quality of life and greatest level of prosperity for its followers. The values, language, rituals, and appropriate behavior supported and promoted by the Church Mountain creates the framework for the fabric of the entire society and culture in which it is implemented. It is of utmost importance that these principles are ones, which will provide the greatest quality of life and highest level of prosperity for the member.

People called to the Church Mountain have a burning desire to influence culture by being the source of values, language, rituals, and appropriate behavior. They are unwavering in their belief of the irrefutability of their value system. When they are moving in their calling, they use their sphere of influence to provide the standard of behavior to govern the interactions between individuals and groups in the other mountains. They are a model for interpersonal relationships and moral character, thus spreading those values and behaviors outside of their usual sphere of influence.

Their purpose is to embody model behavior, and ethics. Moving in the highest level of that calling, they will be careful to be a living testimony to their belief systems and values. A misuse of the influence of the mountain to subject, control or manipulate others will be loathsome to them. They will constantly seek out opportunities to broadcast messages that spread values which build and edify in a truthful manner. In order to do that, they will look for opportunities to support efforts and projects that concentrate on things that are true, noble, right, pure, lovely, admirable, excellent or praiseworthy. When working to alter the perceptions and values of society, especially in those instances when problems are presented or warnings are given, they will be careful to pass on the information in a form that offers hope and a solution. The Church Mountain is called to be the source of solutions. The spread of fear and hopelessness will be avoided at all costs. People called to the Church Mountain are true servants. They have a servant's heart and live to promote the ideals and values of the Church in the other mountains. They will give up their own agendas in an effort to support the greater good of the whole Kingdom structure.

Characteristics of The Church Mountain

- It influences all spheres of society
- It is non-denominational, inter-generational, and is not ethnocentric
- It serves all other mountains or spheres of influence
- It provides the framework for the entire society
- It moves away from the world's values and establishes its own values, language, rituals and appropriate behavior
- Based upon its foundational values and behaviors, it will move out into the world to influence and change conditions to align with those values and behaviors
- Its purpose is to educate members about its principles
- It serves to mature followers and help them to walk in the principles and to display all of the aspects of an adherence to those foundational principles.
- It holds integrity of the message to be of the highest importance
- In its highest form, it draws the true, noble, right, pure, lovely, admirable, excellent or praiseworthy characteristics (Philippians 4:8) out of people.
- Its foundational values should serve to bring the highest level of quality of life and prosperity

FAMILY MOUNTAIN

The Family Mountain

Joshua 24:15 - NLV
*But if you refuse to serve the LORD, then choose today whom you **will**
serve… But as for me and my family, we will serve the LORD.*

Proverbs 11:29 - NIV
*Whoever brings ruin on their family will inherit only wind, and the fool will
be servant to the wise.*

Psalms 103:17 – God's Word Translation
*But from everlasting to everlasting, the LORD's mercy is on those who fear
him. His righteousness belongs to their children and grandchildren,*

From Early Modern English *familie* (not in Middle English), from Latin
familia ("the servants in a household, domestics collectively"), from *famulus*
("servant")/*famula* ("female servant"), from Old Latin *famul*, of obscure
origin - perhaps derived from or cognate to Oscan *famel* ("servant"). Taken
from the old origins of the word, family denotes a group of people whose job
it is to serve others, or one another. The more modern connotation of the
word includes a group of people, who are closely related by blood; who are
related to one another through marriage or more distant blood; or who are
affiliated with one another either through co-habitation or through a shared
purpose or activity, like a Church family.

The family is the primary institution in most societies for the socialization of
children. Within the more narrow definition of the term, most family
organizations are classified by anthropologists as being either matrifocal
(focused on the mother-a mother and her children); conjugal (a husband, his
wife, and children; also called the nuclear family); avuncular (for example, a
grandparent, a brother, his sister, and her children); or extended (parents and
children co-reside with other members of one parent's family). In almost all
societies, the protection and nurturing of children is seen as something of
paramount importance. "Family" can also be used metaphorically to create
more expansive categories such as community, nationhood, global village
and humanism. Within this broader definition, a religious, political or other
"family" serves to educate a junior or new member of a particular group into
the language, values and accepted norms of that group.

During the process of enculturation, people learn the requirements of their surrounding culture and acquire values and behaviors, which are deemed appropriate or necessary within that particular culture. Peers, parents, or other adults will play an important part in the process to limit, direct or shape the individual undergoing socialization. If the process is successful, it will result in competency in the language, values and rituals of the culture. Enculturation can be both deliberate and informal socialization.

Within a family, either in the formal or informal sense, an individual can become an accepted member and fulfill the needed functions and roles of the group through the process of enculturation or socialization. Having undergone that process, the person is taught the recognized norms and values in that group environment. Ultimately, the individual is taught the confines of appropriate conduct, which helps that person to understand the difference between acceptable and unacceptable behavior. Socialization within a family teaches an individual what their role in society is, as well as what appropriate behavior within that society and lifestyle is. Families need to provide a safe environment in which the younger, less-versed members can slowly understand their role in the context of a collective society. The skills necessary to negotiate interpersonal as well as social situations should ideally be passed down within this context as well.

The purpose of a family, the foundation upon which its existence is built, is reflected in the root of the word itself. Families exist to serve. They serve their members by helping them to grow, mature and become the best versions of themselves that they can be. In serving one another they ultimately, from the strength of that unit, reach out to serve others in the wider community as an extension of themselves. A family is a service unit. When that is comprehended, the full benefit to a society, which has family units that are whole, well, and functioning can be understood.

The values, behaviors, social requirements, language and rituals of the culture are not necessarily "created" by the "family". For the most part, they stem from another source outside the household. They are, however, implemented within the family and used as a basis of nurturing and socialization of the newer members. Individual units may, however, develop certain rituals intrinsic and unique to that particular group. The enculturation process would then, of course, include those special values created within that unit. When a family is whole, healthy and functioning, the members socialized within it will reflect that, ensuring its continuation and the continuation of the wider society at the same time.

People called to the Family Mountain have a burning desire to develop and perfect the means and methodology for helping individuals to grow, mature and reach their full potentials. They search for processes that facilitate the passing on of values, behaviors, social requirements, language, and rituals from one group to another individual or group. People called to the Family Mountain seek to foster research into the field of social sciences and human interaction and to develop and perfect existing approaches.

When they are operating in their calling, people in the Family Mountain will use their sphere of influence to help new members of a group to adopt and adapt to the norms and values of that group. They will lead, guide, and speak into their lives as a way to help them grow, mature, and become productive members of the group. They will serve the efforts of the other mountains by preparing these members to step into positions and functions in the other mountains. This will occur through an impartation of the social and emotional skills, helping them to make educated choices in their lives and to be able to interact with others.

Moving in the highest level of that calling, they will be careful to tailor their guidance of the recipient in such a way as to support the development of that person or group. Where they encounter a difficulty with an individual or group, they will adjust their methodologies to facilitate a breakthrough. They are willing to take a backseat to the process and to mold themselves and their message in such a way, that it fits the acclimation style of the individual or group receiving instruction. The person called to the Family Mountain will constantly seek out opportunities to spread values, which build and edify. In order to do that, they will seek to draw out and build the true, noble, right, pure, lovely, admirable, excellent or praiseworthy qualities of a person or group. People called to the Family Mountain are true servants. They have a servant's heart and live to mentor people and groups called to work in all of the other mountains and of the Kingdom. They will give up their own agendas in an effort to support the greater good of the whole structure.

Characteristics of The Family Mountain

- It is universal in nature.
- Its primary function is socialization or enculturation.
- It uses interpersonal relationships in order to pass values, behaviors, social requirements, language, and rituals from one group to another individual or group.
- It seeks to encourage individuals in their maturation process.
- In its highest form, it helps people to embody true, noble, right, pure, lovely, admirable, excellent or praiseworthy characteristics. Philippians 4:8
- It serves to support Kingdom building activities of the other mountains by strengthening the growth and development of the individual members.
- It works to unify the Body by working to develop each member individually, thereby fostering a sense of community and common purpose.
- It is the mountain of service and serves the individual, the group and from the unity of group, all other mountains or spheres of influence.
- It facilitates activities between the different spheres of influence through cooperative value building activities.
- It helps people and groups to identify with and accept unification efforts between the different mountain ranks.
- It builds individual destinies within the divine purpose and structure of society.

EDUCATION MOUNTAIN

The Education Mountain

Proverbs 4:13 - ISV
Hold on to instruction, do not let it go! Guard wisdom, because she is your life!

Proverbs 9:9 - NIV
Instruct the wise and they will be wiser still; teach the righteous and they will add to their learning.

From Middle French *éducation*, from Latin *ēducātiō* ("a breeding, bringing up, rearing"), from *ēdūcō* ("I educate, train"), from *ēdūcō* ("I lead forth, I take out; I raise up, I erect"). Education is the process or art of imparting knowledge, skill and judgment. It is the facts, skills and ideas that have been learned, either formally or informally. Taken together, education requires someone to rear, train, lead someone forth, and to raise someone else up.

In a general sense education is a form of learning in which the knowledge, skills, values, beliefs and habits of a group of people are transferred from one generation to the next, or from one group of individuals to the next through storytelling, discussion, teaching, training, research or interactive media tools. It often takes place under the guidance of others, but learners may also educate themselves. It may also include the transference of information in an informal manner. Any experience that has a formative effect on the way one thinks, feels, or acts may be considered educational. The science and art of how best to teach is called pedagogy.

Traditionally, education has been divided into two types and multiple stages. The types of education are formal and informal. Within formal education there are multiple stages. These stages might include preschool, primary school, and secondary school. At a higher level they could include college, university or apprenticeship. The purpose of a formal education is to teach students within a structured environment. This usually occurs in a school environment where trained teachers teach classrooms of multiple students. The structure of these school systems is primarily designed around a specific set of values or ideals that govern all educational choices within that system. This includes curriculum, physical classroom design, student-teacher interactions, methods of assessment, class size, and educational activities as well as many others.

Within informal education community colleges and specialty schools, offering training in specific skills or arts, provide another avenue for learning for all ages. Additionally, electronic education technology (e-learning) and homeschooling augment other informal learning options to provide the education seeker with many alternatives. Finally, private institutes, coaches and educators are also a means by which to further one's education. Depending upon the culture or area, education may be compulsory up to a certain age. When this age is reached, different systems offer different options for continued education, or require no additional education whatsoever. Some governments have recognized a universal right to education and Article 13 of the United Nations' 1966 International Covenant on Economic, Social and Cultural Rights recognizes the right of everyone to an education.

Education, in and of itself is a neutral entity. It is not inherently positive or negative. Its purpose is to pass on a set of pre-determined values, skills and knowledge from one person to another or from one group to another. Therefore the quality and usefulness of the skills and knowledge passed on depends on the validity of the standards from which they were developed.

The purpose of the Education Mountain, therefore, is to develop and perfect the means and methodology for transferring acquired skills, knowledge and values from one group to another or from one individual to another. It is also to foster research into the field of cognitive learning and to develop and perfect existing tools as well as to search for other means in order to enhance and improve the learning experience.

The quest for additional, innovative educational tools has led to a great boom in e-learning opportunities. Schools, universities, institutes of further education, other centers of learning, online learning platforms, and companies offering electronic teaching tools have and are developing innovative curricula and educational instruments, which are opening doors to people who would not have otherwise been able to participate in further education. These innovations are enabling people of all ages and backgrounds to expand their knowledge base. Even small children and babies have benefitted from this increase in scholastic means and technologies.

Additionally, the Internet has provided an almost limitless source of material for the dedicated scholar. Information, which would have required serious intentional research and endless hours of invested time to gather, can now be found and collected online in a fraction of the time. Libraries are also expanding their electronic presence by offering their catalogs and, in some cases, even scanning and presenting their entire collections online for the benefit of interested parties. This has opened a whole new world of opportunity to process and connect data in a way that would not have been possible only a decade ago. It has also provided possibilities for teachers to interact with students in a different way than has ever been imaginable before. Because technology is increasing and developing exponentially, it remains to be seen which new and innovative educational techniques and products will be available to people in the future.

When they are operating in their calling, people in the Education Mountain will use their sphere of influence to pass information on and to expand the reasoning abilities of the recipients. They will serve the efforts of the other mountains by educating on activities within each of the different spheres. This drive also extends to instructing on issues that encompass more than one sphere of activity. They exist to instruct. Moving in the highest level of that calling, they will be careful to tailor their message to the recipient in such a way as to support the development of that person or group. Where they encounter a difficulty with the assimilation of information, they will adjust their teaching methodologies to facilitate a breakthrough. They are willing to take a backseat to the process and to mold themselves and their message in such a way, that it fits the learning style of the individual or group receiving instruction.

They are champions of truth. In addition to considering truth to be the highest good available, the person called to the Education Mountain will constantly seek out opportunities to spread values, which build and edify. In order to do that, they will seek out material that concentrates on things that are true, noble, right, pure, lovely, admirable, excellent or praiseworthy.

People called to the Education Mountain are true servants. They have a servant's heart and live to instruct and mentor people and groups called to work in all of the other mountains and of the Kingdom. They will give up their own agendas in an effort to support the greater good of the whole structure.

Characteristics of The Education Mountain

- It is universal in nature.
- It seeks to impart knowledge and information.
- It encompasses all forms of traditional education.
- It includes all "modern" forms of education.
- It researches innovations and developments in the other mountains and passes that information on.
- It uses storytelling, discussion, teaching, training and/or research to pass knowledge, skills, values, beliefs and habits from a group of people to others.
- In its highest form, it helps people to identify and think about things that are true, noble, right, pure, lovely, admirable, excellent or praiseworthy. Philippians 4:8
- It serves to support Kingdom building activities of the other mountains by providing instruction and training.
- It works to unify the Body by imparting information on the current situation in different spheres or areas
- It serves all other mountains or spheres of influence.
- It facilitates activities between the different spheres of influence through information exchange.
- It teaches about unification efforts between the different mountain ranks.
- It instructs about the divine purpose and structure of society.

GOVERNMENT MOUNTAIN

The Government Mountain

Proverbs 29:2 – NLT
When the godly are in authority, the people rejoice. But when the wicked are in power, they groan.

Psalm 125:3 – NLT
The wicked will not rule the land of the godly, for then the godly might be tempted to do wrong.

1 Peter 2:13-17 - NASB
13Submit yourselves for the Lord's sake to every human institution, whether to a king as the one in authority, 14or to governors as sent by him for the punishment of evildoers and the praise of those who do right. 15For such is the will of God that by doing right you may silence the ignorance of foolish men. 16Act as free men, and do not use your freedom as a covering for evil, but use it as bond-slaves of God. 17Honor all people, love the brotherhood, fear God, and honor the king.

The term government stems from the Old French gouvernement and from the Latin term gubernatio, which denotes "management and government". It is also a compound formed from the Ancient Greek κυβερνάω (kubernaō, "I steer, drive, guide, pilot") and the Latin -mente, which is the ablative singular form of the word mēns ("mind"). So, taken together, the word government denotes a management system designed to guide or steer the minds of mankind.

Governments are political systems and institutions that exist to impose a set of ideological principals uniformly and on a wide scale. Those systems and institutions create an overreaching hierarchy, which constitutes the organization of that government. Governments of all kinds currently affect every human activity in many important ways. Therefore it is imperative, that the ideological principals applied as well as the hierarchical structure used be chosen wisely and with diligence, so that the resulting societal structure and values serve the widest possible constituency.

There are a number of different forms of government. For the most part they can be classified into two types. The first type are those in which the power to impose ideological principles is concentrated in the hands of a single person. These governmental forms are: autocracy, despotism, dictatorship and fascism. Historically, the challenge in these systems of government is making sure that the individual, in whom the power is concentrated, does not develop psychological or sociological problems, which would result in power being used to the detriment of those being led, as opposed to being used to their benefit. The degeneration of these systems follows in the order in which they have been listed. For example: an autocrat needs servants while a despot needs slaves.

The second type of government forms are those in which the power to impose and enforce ideological principles is concentrated in the hands of a certain group of people. These are primarily: aristocracy, geniocracy, kratocracy, meritocracy, and timocracy. They also include oligarchy and plutocracy, technocracy, and democracy. Starting at the top of the list an aristocracy is a government by the "best" people; a geniocracy is a rule by the intelligent; a kratocracy is a government by the strong. A meritocracy is a system of governance where groups are selected on the basis of people's ability, knowledge in a given area, and contributions to society.

Governments exist to implement a chosen set of values. If the value set is agreed upon, a functioning government will apply those values and enforce those values at all levels of society. Governmental systems are neutral entities. As long as the creation of the value system and the implementation of those values are separated, governmental structures will serve the purpose that they are designed for. It is when the government begins to develop and implement a set of its own values, or when the originator of values within a society begins to step into and create a structure to implement those values, that society will degenerate into a system which harms the people it was created to serve.

Essentially, the form of government is irrelevant. Each and every system of governance can be utilized to achieve the purpose of implementing a system of values on a wide scale. The most important thing is that the foundational system of values for a society is generated outside of the structure of governance. Ultimately, it is the quality of those values that the governmental system enforces and spreads, which will determine if the society is one that will benefit the populace, or one which will undermine the very fabric of that society itself.

People who are called to the Government Mountain have a burning desire to implement a chosen set of values and norms through the broadest and most universal means possible. The focus of those people is to initiate or use a system of structure and hierarchy in order to manage and guide the behaviors of others with a view towards adopting those values and norms. When they are moving in their calling, people in the Government Mountain will use their sphere of influence to systematically apply a set of ideological principles on a wide scale. They will serve the efforts of the other mountains by providing the legislative and governmental framework necessary to allow people in those mountains to pursue activities without unnecessary hindrances.

They exist to create and steward overreaching hierarchies, which provide organization and structure to a society or system. The people in the Government Mountain are called to implement universal rules of behaviors, which regulate the workings of societies, organizations, and the people living and working in them. When operating in the highest level of that calling, they will seek out universal governing principles as the basis of their governance, which inspires and supports things that are true, noble, right, pure, lovely, admirable, excellent or praiseworthy.

A true Government Mountain person will never misuse their position to gain unfair advantage over the others within the system. They will adhere to the laws, rules and by laws that they have established and are enforcing. A dual system in which there is a system of governance for the masses with a separate system of rules for themselves will be loathsome to people called to this mountain.

People called to the Government Mountain are true servants. They have a servant's heart and live to give structure and direction to societies and groups, thereby promoting the activities of the other mountains and of the Kingdom. They will give up their own agendas in an effort to support the greater good of the whole structure. The people called to the Government Mountain have an indispensible role to play in bringing the Kingdom to Earth.

Characteristics of The Government Mountain

- It can be local, regional, national and global in nature.
- It organizes and manages the workings of society.
- It includes all traditional and "modern" governance models.
- Its purpose is to implement a set of predetermined values on a wide scale.
- The values to be implemented within the governmental structure must come from a source outside the government itself. This must be a "higher" source.
- In its highest form, it helps people to live under a societal structure, which supports things that are true, noble, right, pure, lovely, admirable, excellent or praiseworthy. Philippians 4:8
- It works together with other mountains to clarify and adjust the values that are to be implemented.
- It serves all other mountains or spheres of influence.
- It is the vehicle through which all other mountains receive the structure and form for the implementation of the value set.
- It facilitates activities between the different spheres of influence through a common purpose.
- It unifies efforts between the different mountain ranks, because it is an instrument for wide-scale reformation.
- It serves as a vehicle to implement the values inherent in the divine purpose for and structure of society.

BUSINESS MOUNTAIN

The Business Mountain

Exodus 20:25 - NIV
"If you lend money to one of my people among you who is needy, do not treat it like a business deal; charge no interest."

Luke 19:15 - NASB
"It happened when he had come back again, having received the kingdom, that he commanded these servants, to whom he had given the money, to be called to him, that he might know what they had gained by conducting business."

Acts 6:3 - KJV
Therefore select from among you, brothers, seven men of good report, full of the Holy Spirit and of wisdom, whom we may appoint over this business.

James 4:13-17 - NASB
13Come now, you who say, "Today or tomorrow we will go to such and such a city, and spend a year there and engage in business and make a profit." 14Yet you do not know what your life will be like tomorrow. You are just a vapor that appears for a little while and then vanishes away. 15Instead, you ought to say, "If the Lord wills, we will live and also do this or that." 16But as it is, you boast in your arrogance; all such boasting is evil. 17Therefore, to one who knows the right thing to do and does not do it, to him it is sin.

The meaning of the term business is equivalent to the combination of busy + -ness. The term busy stems from the Middle English busi, besy, bisi, from the Old English bysiġ, *biesiġ, bisiġ ("busy, occupied, diligent"), from the Proto-Germanic *bisigaz ("diligent; zealous; busy"). Cognate with the Dutch bezig ("busy"), Low German besig ("busy"), Old Frisian bisgia ("to use"), Old English bisgian ("to occupy, employ, trouble, afflict").

The suffix –ness stems from the Old English –nes, which is of Germanic origin, and related to the Gothis –nassus and denotes a state, condition, or quality, or an instance of one of these. Taken together, the term business is the condition, quality or status of being occupied, employed and diligent. It is the situation of being useful. Businesses are intended to be structures, which offer goods and services to customers. These products are meant to be beneficial, wholesome and useful for the customers.

There are many diverse types of business and they can be classified into nine different categories. These are:

1. Agriculture and mining – produce raw materials
2. Financial – concentrate on the investment and management of capital
3. Information – support the sale of intellectual property, which includes movie studios, publishers and internet and software companies
4. Manufacturers – produce products
5. Real Estate – sell, rent and develop properties
6. Retailers and distributors – act as middlemen and connect the manufacturers with their intended consumers
7. Service – offer intangible goods or services
8. Transportation – deliver products and people
9. Utilities – produce public services such as water, electricity, and waste management. This is usually mandated through a government charter.

A business, also known as an enterprise or a firm, is an organization involved in the trade of goods, services or both, to consumers. In the highest sense, the activity of business is called to place the value and helpfulness of products to the customer above the profit motivation. In most cases, businesses are privately owned. They may also be not-for-profit or state-owned. Businesses, which are owned by multiple individuals, are usually referred to as companies. Business can also refer to a particular organization or, more generally, to an entire market sector. There are compound forms of the term business, which refer to subsets of the word's broader meaning, such as Eco business. These compound terms are used to designate all activity by suppliers of goods and services within that sub-sector of the market.

One of the ultimate goals of commerce is to have a particular enterprise generate more turnover in sales than it has in expenditures. This would yield a profit. Although this is an important part of commerce, ultimately it should not overshadow the service aspect of the economic sector. The prime motivation of any commercial enterprise should be to serve the public and the Earth, by providing goods and services that cover a particular need.

People called to the Business Mountain have a burning desire to bring products and services to people. Their focus is to locate innovative and creative products and services and carry them to the point of production and distribution to the widest possible customer base. When they are moving in their calling, people in the Business Mountain will use their sphere of influence to serve the activities of the other mountains by looking for ways to provide products and services that will aide them. They will also actively invest in research and development, perfecting already existing merchandise.

They exist to transform ideas into reality. Moving in the highest level of that calling, they will be careful to only support and promote goods and services that serve the highest possible good of the client and of the world in general. A misuse of the power of business to create and distribute products and services that do not support and promote the good of the customer or, on a wider level, the health and well-being of the planet as a whole, will be loathsome to a true business mountain person.

In the area of finances, Kingdom people called to this aspect of business will have a strong dislike of any products, services or tactics used solely for the purpose of increasing profits. The manipulation of financial instruments and the tactic of playing with timing and rates will be loathsome to a Kingdom Business Mountain person. Reformers called to this mountain will seek to develop the means to reform the system. Revelators will be inclined to leak information, which would expose corruption in the system. Proclaimers will carry a message of the necessity for change. Nurturers will seek to promote wholeness within the system and the Educators will research and educate on alternatives to the current methodology.

In addition to considering the well being of the customer to be the highest good available, the person called to the Business Mountain will constantly seek out opportunities to promote goods and services that spread values, which build and edify. In order to do that, they will seek out merchandise to advance, which concentrates on things that are true, noble, right, pure, lovely, admirable, excellent or worthy of praise. People called to the Business Mountain are true servants. They have a servant's heart and live to promote innovation in products and services developed in the other mountains and of the Kingdom. They will give up their own agendas in an effort to support the greater good of the whole structure. The people called to the Business Mountain have an indispensible role to play in bringing the Kingdom to Earth.

Characteristics of The Business Mountain

- It can be both local and global in nature
- It supports the innovation of products and services
- It encompasses all forms of traditional business
- It includes all "modern" forms of business
- It seeks to foster innovation in all spheres of influence
- Its purpose is to better the condition of the world and humanity through the creation, production and distribution of innovative products and services
- In its highest form, it helps people to create and produce things that are true, noble, right, pure, lovely, admirable, excellent or praiseworthy. Philippians 4:8
- It serves to support the Kingdom building activities of the other mountains through the production and distribution of products and services
- It works to unify the Church by servicing needs in different spheres or areas
- It serves all other mountains or spheres of influence by financing their business endeavors
- It is the vehicle through which all other mountains distribute their innovations
- It unifies efforts between the different mountain ranks by facilitating unilateral distribution of innovations
- It supports the expansion of the divine purpose and structure of society by spreading products and services that reflect Kingdom culture

ARTS & ENTERTAINMENT
MOUNTAIN

The Arts & Entertainment Mountain

Ecclesiastes 3:4 - NIV
a time to weep and a time to laugh, a time to mourn and a time to dance,

Exodus 35:35 - NIV
He has filled them with skill to do all kinds of work as engravers, designers, embroiderers in blue, purple and scarlet yarn and fine linen, and weavers-- all of them skilled workers and designers.

Psalm 150:1-6 - NASB
1 Praise the LORD! Praise God in His sanctuary; Praise Him in His mighty expanse. 2 Praise Him for His mighty deeds; Praise Him according to His excellent greatness. 3 Praise Him with trumpet sound; Praise Him with harp and lyre. 4 Praise Him with timbrel and dancing; Praise Him with stringed instruments and pipe. 5 Praise Him with loud cymbals; Praise Him with resounding cymbals. 6 Let everything that has breath praise the LORD. Praise the LORD!

The word art comes from the Middle English *art*, from the Old French *art*, and from the Latin *artem*. It has many different meanings. Art is the conscious production or arrangement of sounds, colors, forms, movements, or other elements in a manner that causes a response in the senses and emotions. This can be accomplished through the production of the beautiful in a graphic or plastic medium or it can be a skillful creative activity that has an aesthetic focus. Art is the study and the product of the creative processes as well as a field or category of these creative processes such as painting, sculpture, music, ballet, or literature. The aesthetic value of something is called art. Art is also the body of works produced, which carry that aesthetic value. Finally, "the art of" something denotes a skill that is attained by study, practice or observation. Art represents an outlet of expression that is usually influenced by culture, which, in turn helps to change culture. It is a documented expression of a sentient being through or on an accessible medium so that anyone can view, hear or experience it. Art is the physical manifestation of the internal creative impulse.

Major constituents of the arts include literature (poetry, novels, short stories, and epics); performing arts (music, dance, and theatre); culinary arts (cooking, baking, working with chocolate, and winemaking); media arts like photography and cinematography, and visual arts (drawing, painting, and sculpting). Some art forms are a combination of different art forms. Film, for example, is a combination of performance art and media art. And comics are a combination of visual arts and literature.

The word entertainment comes from the Old French entretenement and entretenir, from entre ("among") and tenir ("to hold"), and from the Latin inter and *teneō* ("hold, keep"). Taken together, entertainment is an activity designed to give pleasure, enjoyment, diversion, amusement, or relaxation to an audience, regardless of the level of personal participation of the audience. Entertainment can be passive, as in the case of going to the theater or a movie, or it can be active, when the audience is participating in games or other activities. It can also be the act of developing and putting on a show for the enjoyment or amusement of others.

The purpose of entertainment is to create an activity that holds the attention and interest of an audience; that gives pleasure or delight; or offers relaxation or recreation. People have the capacity of viewing any idea or task as entertaining. Despite the difference in preference, most current forms of entertainment are forms that have developed over thousands of years specifically for the purpose of capturing an audience's attention. Storytelling, music, drama, dance and other types of performance exist in all cultures and have developed at a rapid rate through the entertainment industry, which has fostered the evolution by recording and selling products.

Entertainment evolves and can be adapted to suit any scale, ranging from an individual choosing private entertainment from a now enormous array of pre-recorded products; to a dinner-theater adaptation for two; to any size or type of party that includes music and dance; to performances intended for thousands; and those designed to impact a global audience. The familiar forms of entertainment have the capacity to cross over different media and have demonstrated a seemingly unlimited potential for creative remix. This has ensured the continuity and longevity of many themes, images, and structures. Additionally, modern trends have produced a new form of entertainment through the staging of the work of others. Activities, which were once considered to be work, such as cooking, construction or even voice development, have become entertainment through the advent of reality television.

Most forms of entertainment have persisted and evolved over many centuries. They have changed and developed primarily due to changes in culture, technology and fashion. Although there are newer forms of media entertainment like video games, Internet gaming, DVD's etc., the innovative forms continue to tell stories, present drama and to play music. Film, music or dance festivals also provide opportunities for art-induced entertainment. Amusement has become synonymous for entertainment, in recent times. Although fun and laughter can be a form of entertainment, the highest form of the craft involves creating a way to encourage an audience to grow, achieving insight or intellectual development. It is when the serious side of entertainment is explored, that advancement and progress result. Arts and entertainment provide a means for advancing creativity and innovation and bringing it to the public to act as a catalyst for societal development, growth and maturation.

People called to the Arts & Entertainment Mountain have a burning desire to create and spread unique expressions of creativity and innovation and to assist others in entertainment and recreation activities. Their focus is to support the creation of all things beautiful and innovative and they will use every means possible to be a catalyst for change and progress in society. When they are moving in their calling, people in the Arts and Entertainment Mountain will use their sphere of influence to create vehicles for change and transformation. They will also serve the efforts of the other mountains to solve their problems by encouraging creativity, innovation and out-of-the-box thinking. This drive also extends to working together with others, who are active in different spheres of influence, to foster synergy as a basis for innovative thinking.

They exist to promote originality and to encourage work/life balance through recreation and entertainment. Moving in the highest level of that calling, they will create works of art and recreational experiences that spread values, which build and edify.

In order to do that, they will concentrate on things that are true, noble, right, pure, lovely, admirable, excellent or praiseworthy. They will also support entertainment and artistic efforts, which challenge entrenched forms of thinking by presenting works promoting changes in insight and expansion of intellectual growth.

Characteristics of The Arts and Entertainment Mountain

- It can be both local and global in nature.
- It broadens the horizons of people.
- It encompasses all forms of traditional and modern
- arts & entertainment.
- It is an avenue for creativity to be introduced to society.
- It provides amusement and recreation to people.
- In its highest form, it helps people to identify, grow from or birth things that are true, noble, right, pure, lovely, admirable, excellent or praiseworthy. Philippians 4:8
- It supports human development and improvement, by offering a space for innovation, creativity and recreation.
- It encourages development and innovation in the other mountains by acting as a catalyst for change.
- It serves all other mountains or spheres of influence.
- It is the vehicle through which ingenuity is released into the other mountains and the Kingdom.
- It facilitates activities between the different spheres of influence through cooperative creative efforts.
- It unifies society by providing unusual vehicles to present the concept of the divine purpose and structure of society.

MEDIA
MOUNTAIN

The Media Mountain

Proverbs 25:25 - NIV
Like cold water to a weary soul is good news from a distant land.

Isaiah 52:7 - NASB
How lovely on the mountains Are the feet of him who brings good news, Who announces peace And brings good news of happiness, Who announces salvation, And says to Zion, "Your God reigns!"

Daniel 12:4 - ESV
"But you, Daniel, shut up the words and seal the book, until the time of the end. Many shall run to and fro, and knowledge shall increase."

Media is the plural form of the word medium. Medium is one of the means or channels of general communication, information, or entertainment in society, such as newspapers, radio or television. Media denotes the collective communication outlets or tools that are used to store and deliver information or data. It is either associated with communication media, or the specialized communication businesses such as: print media and the press, photography, advertising, cinema, broadcasting (radio and television) and/or publishing.

Both words Media (plural) or medium (singular) denote overreaching forms of mass communication. The word *communication* comes from the Latin root *communicare*. *Communicare* means to join with, to receive, and to take a share of. So, in total, media or mass media are systems that allow people to connect with others in experiencing something, that allow people to receive information or that allow people to partake of something.

Over the course of the last century, telecommunications and mass media have improved and developed to such an extent, that it is now possible to simultaneously reach millions upon millions of people around the globe. This has happened through the development of the Internet, email, Internet forums and teleportation platforms that use satellite to broadcast globally.

In addition to this, there have been massive advancements in many traditional broadcast media and mass media forms. These advancements have been partially due to improvements in technology and primarily due to the use of the advancements in other forms of media, which has enabled them to piggyback. As a result, they are now able to reach a far greater audience than they were even a few years ago. Television, cinema, radio, newspapers, and magazines are now able to impact a globe-spanning audience, where this would have been impossible only twenty years ago.

Because of innovations in electronic technology, media devices have been shrinking both in size and in cost. This has made them increasingly affordable, even for the most impoverished in the world. A whole new world of potential expansion for the Media Mountain has opened up as a result of this advancement in technology. People called to the Media Mountain have a great opportunity to take advantage of the opportunities available, if they recognize them.

Communication has become much easier through improvements in media technology. Today even the youngest of children are able to use media tools and are expected to have a general understanding of the various technologies available by the time they enter into the schooling system. The Internet is arguably one of the most effective tools for communication through mass media today. Media outlets such as e-mail, Skype, Facebook as well as online communities have brought people closer together and created new avenues for quickly reaching large global audiences.

There is a great deal of power, which rests in the ability to transfer a message to many people very quickly. Power is a neutral entity. It can be used for a good purpose, or it can be used to harm. Used for a positive purpose and in a positive manner, the power of mass media can serve others by providing a platform to showcase unusual and creative solutions and events in all of the other mountains. It can build up, it can support and it can move these efforts further and faster, than they could ever have managed themselves.

The advancements in mass media have helped to connect diverse people from various geographical locations. They could also help create a better world, if put in the hands of a people called to work with them and determined to do just that.

People called to the Media Mountain have a burning desire to broadcast information and entertainment. Their focus is to seek out pertinent material or things of interest and to use any and every means possible to bring those to as many people as possible. When they are moving in their calling, people in the Media Mountain will use their sphere of influence to inform about the activities of the other mountains. They will serve the efforts of the other mountains by educating on activities within each of the different spheres. This drive also extends to instructing on events that encompass more than one sphere of activity. They exist to spread news. Moving in the highest level of that calling, they will be careful to examine the facts and disperse only that information, which has been determined to be the truth. A misuse of the power of media to misinform and manipulate the public will be loathsome to a true media mountain person.

In addition to considering truth to be the highest good available, the person called to the Media Mountain will constantly seek out opportunities to broadcast messages that spread values which build and edify. In order to do that, they will seek out events or entertainment, which concentrates on things that are true, noble, right, pure, lovely, admirable, excellent or praiseworthy. When disseminating information designed to present problems or to warn, they will be careful to weigh all sides of the issue and will present that necessary material in a form that offers hope and a solution in addition to educating on the difficulty. The spread of fear and hopelessness will be avoided at all costs.

The Media Mountain is the last in the row of mountains. It has the function of being the informer of the activities of the other mountains. As such, it is the greatest servant in the Kingdom structure (Matthew 20:16). And it is designed to be the greatest of the mountains through its service to the other mountains (Matthew 20:26, 23:11; Luke 22:26). In the world, this order has been reversed. Because of this, the world's Media Mountain has supplanted all other mountains in its power and influence. The coming of the Kingdom to Earth will bring the mountains back into their proper order.

Characteristics of The Media Mountain

- It can be both local and global in nature
- It seeks to disseminate information
- It encompasses all forms of traditional communication
- It includes all "modern" forms of communication
- It seeks to locate events of interest in the other mountains
- Its purpose is to disseminate information about the activities in the other mountains
- In its highest form, it helps people to identify and think about things that are true, noble, right, pure, lovely, admirable, excellent or praiseworthy. Philippians 4:8
- It serves to support, through information dissemination, the Kingdom building activities of the other mountains
- It works to unify the Church by spreading information on the current situation in different spheres or areas
- It serves all other mountains or spheres of influence
- It is the vehicle through which all other mountains spread knowledge
- It facilitates activities between the different spheres of influence through information exchange
- It unifies efforts between the different mountain ranks
- It serves as a vehicle to spread knowledge about the divine purpose and structure of society

The Mountain Order

Each individual Mountain or Sphere of Influence has a God ordained role to fulfill in society and every single one of them is vital to the efficient functioning of The Kingdom. In addition to that, each Sphere of Influence is uniquely called to solve a problem and has a function. Like the Ranks, there is no sphere of influence that is more (or less) important than the other. And, as in the case of the Ranks, the Mountains in God's Kingdom design are dependent on one another. And the primary duty of each Mountain is to serve the other Mountains. By serving the others, each Mountain will help them to fulfill their callings within the Kingdom structure.

As I was introduced to God's design for society, the thing that impressed me the most was the fact that these functions were interdependent. No Mountain could exist and complete its assignment without the cooperation and support of the others. The Mountains are not islands. Just as no Rank can exist outside of a collective of the others, so no Mountain can complete its true function without interacting with the other Mountains. God's Kingdom design is a system of interdependence, not one of independence.

Like an intricately woven tapestry, every Mountain is connected to the others. Also, every Mountains purpose is vital for the smooth functioning of the whole system. Without getting too detailed, here is an example. Within the Kingdom the Business Mountain has the function of being the clearinghouse for useful ideas. People within this mountain will search the other Mountains for products and services that are useful, beneficial, and do no harm to the Earth or to the customers who will buy those products and services. Once a needed product or service is found, the Business Mountain then has the job to develop manufacturing and distribution systems so that those products and services get to the people that need them in the most efficient manner possible. The products and services do not come out of the Business Mountain; they come out of the other mountains. The job of the Business Mountain is to search for innovations, or to recognize needs within the other mountains and then to get the products and services to those that need it.

The Business Mountain is the distributor of products and services; it is not the originator. This makes the mountain completely dependent upon the others for ideas and products. Without the innovations from within the other mountains, the Business Mountain would not exist. It could not function. Doing business is simply a way of serving the Body of Christ by helping people who need something by giving them what they need. This is a far cry from the way in which business is currently conducted under the world's system.

The problem with society today is that those working in the Mountains have no idea what the underlying God-given functions of the Mountains are. In addition to that, those functions are currently being perverted. And the perversion is so all-encompassing that one could say that the order of the mountains has been flipped on its head. Where the primary place of importance, according to God's design, should be the Church Mountain, it has slipped to the lowest place in modern society. And, where the Media Mountain should be last and servant to all of the other Mountains, it has taken the prominent position of importance within society. This contradiction as well as the original design intent of The Kingdom will be examined at length in Chapter Seven.

---

[1] Jeynes, Dr. William, "God, China & Capitalism: Is Christianity in China the Key Ingredient for Economic Success?", at Family Research Council in Washington, DC., Tuesday, May 17, 2011. Cited in Vu, Michelle A., "Scholar: China Notices Link Between Christianity, U.S. Economic Success", The Christian Post, May 18, 2011.

[2] Weber, Max, *The Protestant Ethic and the Spirit of Capitalism*, transl. Peter Baehr and Gordon C. Wells, Penguin Books, 2002.

[3] Mangalwadi, Vishal, *The Book that Made Your World: How the Bible Created the Soul of Western Civilization*, Thomas Nelson, 2011.

God's Battle Plan
for Dominion

Chapter Seven – God's Battle Plan

Now that you have seen the pieces to the Kingdom structure, it is time to examine how those pieces work together. It was very interesting to me, to experience the way in which The King showed me His Kingdom construction. I have a very logical mind. I like to start things at the beginning and work them through from start to finish. Architects are like that. For the most part, we work in terms of projects. Every project has a beginning and middle. In my opinion, however, the most important thing is the end. When you have finished something and you can stand back and admire the work that has been done. To me, that is the most important thing.

It certainly must have been a similar experience for God, when He stood back after having spent six days creating the Earth and beheld what He had created. The Bible says that He looked and saw that it was very good (Genesis 1:31). In an interesting aside, God didn't start patting himself on the back until the end of the third day. It was then that He started to see His plan coming together and He liked what He was seeing. I guess the work of the first two days didn't give enough of an impression of the final product.

When I started receiving the revelation of God's Kingdom design He began by rolling it out backwards. The first nudge was the fact that the five-fold was the core element of His design and that every person on the planet, regardless of the mountain that they were called to influence, functioned in one of these five roles. I was staying with Rebecca Rhodes at the time and when I dropped that one on her, she was stunned. In her typical way, she just said, "I need some time to process that one". Then, as the details of each rank's function were revealed, we both realized the wisdom of the design. We also began to look at all of the people around us with a view towards trying to determine which of the ranks each of them held. We did the same with the roles of actors in movies and in television shows. The thought was that this design must be true regardless of church affiliation or belief structure. If it is a universal law, it must apply to everyone, everywhere, so the line of reasoning went. And it was. It became a game to us. We would sit in front of the television and watch an episode of a well-known television series and ask each other, "So what rank does 'so-and-so' have?" This exercise helped hone our ability to recognize each of the functions. We also gained a greater understanding of the depth of the different functions by doing these analyses. It was like a type of guessing game.

After the ranks with their roles and functions in the Kingdom were revealed. The Lord began to reveal the purposes and functions of the different mountains or spheres of influence. This was a little more complicated. I often had to stop and spend considerable time in prayer to truly grasp the role of each one and how they interacted with one another. The most amazing thing was that, once again, The Lord rolled the revelations out backwards. Well, at least backwards in terms of Kingdom structure. Forwards, if you view it from the perspective of the world's way of doing things.

God began revealing His Kingdom structure, by talking about the media mountain. Currently, in the world's system, this mountain is the most important. In the Kingdom structure, however, it is dead last on the list. It took me some time to understand why. When the enemy hijacks a design from God, he mimics it, but perverts and twists it in the process. What God intended to bless, the enemy will use to curse. This is the reason that the mountain hierarchy has effectively been flipped on its head. After that, one by one, God revealed the purpose of the other mountains. As I climbed the ladder of mountain hierarchy, I began to understand the overall structure of the Kingdom. With each successive mountain, the complexity, the majesty, and the genius of the design became more apparent. I often had to stop, when the scope of the download became too much for me, or, when I didn't quite grasp a certain point.

When I graduated from university the first time, I graduated with a major in the field of Architecture - Building Technologies. I also graduated with a slew of minors. Among those was a minor in History with a special focus on Church History. I have always had a love of history, so to me adding an extra year of studies in order to get those minors wasn't a burden; it was a pleasure. Now, faced with the daunting task of trying to understand the complexity of God's design for His Kingdom, I began to grasp why that extra year of study had been necessary. My foray into the world of history had given me the foundation of knowledge necessary to recognize how the different mountains had been used and misused throughout the centuries in order to change the course and destiny of nations. Without that background in history, I'm not sure that I would have been able to connect the dots. Reading this book, you will benefit from my education, because I am going to use two well-known periods in world history to illustrate how the Kingdom functions. I hope that the examples will make the whole structure more visible and more understandable.

The Kingdom Mountain – Command Central

I had heard about the Seven Mountain message. In the research that I had done on the subject, I realized that there was an original message and then that others had received additional clarification of the spheres of influence over the years. I also understood that each of these spheres was considered to be independent from one another. The idea that they have a hierarchy was new to me. The next surprise was that there is actually an eighth mountain.

This revelation caused a lot of soul-searching within Rebecca, her team at ILD, and myself. When I found the Bible verses supporting the idea, I had no reason to question any longer. Some of the others, however, needed more time. That is, until someone recognized that it hadn't been possible to reveal the presence of the eighth mountain before then and the lack of awareness of the Seven Mountain message among the Body of Christ was the cause of that. It is not possible to populate that eighth mountain, until enough people are in the other seven first. The eighth mountain, the Kingdom Mountain, is command central of the End-Times army.

After I had received the general organizational scheme of the Kingdom from The Lord, Rebecca and I developed a battery of tests to help people quickly determine their place in that structure. Following a scientific course of validation, ILD and I then started Beta testing the assessments within groups. One of the questions, repeatedly asked by the participants, was why there were no sample occupations given for the Kingdom mountain ranks.

I couldn't answer that question. So I turned to the only one who could. The picture I got was a trench in a war, I wasn't sure if it was WWI or WWII, and a group of men. They were using a field telephone. You know, the kind that you have to crank to get to work. The turning of the crank generates the electricity needed for the telephone to work. After I saw the field telephone, I recognized that it could only have been WWII, since those telephones have only been used in the wars following the First World War.

The interpretation of that picture answered the question I had. Kingdom people are on the front lines of the spiritual war for dominion on Earth. On the front lines, there are no clearly defined job descriptions. There is no set plan of engagement. People on the front lines of a battle have to be the most flexible people in any war. They need to be able to react to situations quickly, without hesitation. They need to be able to stop whatever they are doing, move to a more advantageous position and be adaptable enough to do exactly whatever the situation requires them to do.

The only possible thing that would give a front-line fighter in a war an advantage is intelligence. Not just any kind of intelligence. Immediate, accurate, and direct information from a credible and superior source that is provided exactly where they are, offers them the needed advantage over their enemy. It is the difference between victory and defeat in the battle. The field telephone represents the lifeline of a front-line fighter in the war over dominion. The telephone connects the fighters with the intelligence source, and that source is the Father. The single most important skill that a Kingdom person can develop is their ability to accurately hear and discern the information being given to them by the King and the Holy Spirit.

There can be no sample occupations for a person called to the Kingdom Mountain because that person is a front-line fighter in a war. The position requires extreme flexibility and, more importantly, the position requires extreme obedience. Although all Christians are called to crucify their flesh and submit to the Lordship of Jesus, the front-line fighters in the Kingdom Mountain must achieve this with a much greater level of maturity. It is imperative that they understand this. Yielding to the flesh, when you hold this position in the Kingdom, can cause casualties. Because the level of authority in the Kingdom Mountain is a higher one, the casualties are not just restricted to a single individual. Should a Kingdom person yield to the flesh and step away from submission to the King, the resulting damage could cause many to fall and lead to great losses in the battle.

The Kingdom Mountain has a coordinating function in the battle for influence on Earth. It serves to promote unity among the mountains by connecting individuals or efforts in the specific mountains together. The synergy developed by creating mountain-spanning initiatives increases the effect of individual endeavors. Ranks in this mountain are commissioned by the King to be servants to all of the other mountains, because they serve individual initiatives within them when necessary. Kingdom mountain servants go where they are led by the Holy Spirit to serve. They are highly flexible and adaptable individuals. Their loyalty, service, and obedience are directed toward the King and the growth and development of His Kingdom on Earth above all else.

How the Ranks Work Together

The ranks, while depicted as hierarchical, are not positions of promotion. Each one has a distinct function, which must be fulfilled regardless of their physical location or their sphere of influence. Within the Kingdom, ranks are job descriptions. In order to create a highly effective, functioning unit, each one of the ranks must be present within a grouping. The Kingdom was designed as a system of interdependence. While it is possible for ranks to function independently and outside of a grouping of five, the greatest successes will be achieved when all of them work together. Advances and breakthroughs will be the result when that group of five, termed the "Fab Five" by Rebecca Rhodes, operates within the same mountain or sphere of influence and with a view towards the same goal.

In an encounter with The Holy Spirit, I was told that when a group of all five ranks come together and there is unity among the group with respect to the purpose and individual functions within the group, that unity would create a synergy. That synergy, in turn, would create an environment in which a 300% increase in effectiveness and efficiency is achieved. This is in comparison to efforts that do not have all five ranks operating in unity towards a purpose.

Reformers

The job of the Reformer within the group of five is to identify the changes that need to be made and to challenge the others in the group to begin to implement those changes. This does not mean that the Reformer is seeking change for change's sake. Instead, the primary motivating factor of a

Reformer is to bring people, situations, organizations, cities, regions, nations or any other entity into alignment with their God- ordained purpose. They are called to unstick stuck systems and help people, who are stuck in their lives, move forward again. For the most part, Reformers are equipped with a keen sense of discernment, which allows them to recognize the will of God for those that they are trying to lead down a path of change. Reformers are the leaders in the group of five; they give direction. It is for this reason, that the rank of Reformer was listed first in Ephesians 4.

This does not mean that all projects, efforts or initiatives must be under the leadership of Reformers. Each rank, when utilizing its particular skills and talents and carried by a born-again believer, is capable of carrying a leadership role. A Reformer, who is working out of the Kingdom Mountain, will humble themselves, come alongside the initiative of another Mountain, submit to the leadership of the group and offer guidance and assistance to that initiative. What the leader of an initiative, who is not a Reformer, must understand is that the Reformer in his or her group has the DNA necessary to chart a course through the rugged terrain, and bring the effort to a successful finish. Any one of the other ranks may have the position of leader in a group, but a wise leader will utilize the God-given gifts of the Reformer as those gifts were intended. Anything less will cause friction and frustration within the group.

Revelators

Where Reformers see what needs to be changed and challenge the other ranks to move with them in doing it, Revelators give the specifics of what needs to happen and how to achieve that. The Reformer will chart the course; the Revelator provides the real-time information needed to navigate the initiative through the obstacles on that course. This cooperation can help the Reformer glean accurate up-to-date information on the mission. In turn, this assures the most effective implementation of the overall plan. Revelators are the navigators that will recognize hindrances and obstacles before the others. It is that keen sense of insight that will assist the group as it moves forward along a path to reach its objectives.

The Revelator will always profit from cooperation with a Reformer, because the Reformer will help the Revelator to remain goal orientated. This will help insure that "self" is kept out of the project. Revelators are also assets to the other members of the initiative. They assist the Proclaimer by giving real-time accurate information and providing details about the thing that the Proclaimer is "selling" and they can be great assets to Nurturers once a relationship has developed between them. Revelators can help them recognize things they might have overlooked, because of their close proximity to the situation. Educators receive hints from them to help them find the answers they are seeking. These will then be able to deliver greater truths and an expanded understanding as a result.

When facing issues of conflict or ethical issues stemming from within the group, the Revelator has the ability to accurately discern what the problem is, the cause of the problem, and the parties involved in that problem. It is part of the Revelators role as navigator to offer accurate insight into challenges facing the group. It is also the job of the Revelator to relay rebukes from the King, when those become necessary. For a mature believer, these situations are highly uncomfortable. Submission to the King of the Kingdom sometimes calls us to do things that we find painful or that cause us to stretch.

Proclaimers

Proclaimers are the salespeople and cheerleaders of any job. They were given the gift of being able to spread a message economically and effectively. Within the group of five, when Proclaimers are given the task of selling something, they will instinctively know the best and most impactful method to use in order to accomplish that task. They are most successful, when they are completely convinced of the thing they are trying to sell people on. Because of this they are energetic and very enthusiastic. They can also tend to be loud.

Their second task in a five-fold team is to spread enthusiasm. Every group will be faced with times in which the motivation to continue wanes. In these moments, it is the job of the Proclaimer to remind everyone of why they joined the group in the first place.

It is important for a Proclaimer to find a team comprised of the other four ranks. This is necessary, so that the Proclaimer maintains the integrity of the message that he or she is called to carry. Working together with a Revelator will help the Proclaimer receive accurate up-to-date information on the message. The Proclaimer will help Nurturers to stay focused and keep motivated, as the Nurturer can sometimes get caught up in the details of the emotional/relationship aspect of the overall plan. Proclaimers can also support the work of the Educator by providing tangible results from the research done on particular topics. Reformers need the enthusiasm of Proclaimers to help them keep motivated.

Nurturers

The Nurturer's job, within a five-fold team, is to help each member of the team to gain, retain, and maintain wholeness. Group dynamics can often be strenuous. Therefore it is imperative that any serious group effort includes one member of this rank. Nurturers often walk in keen relational discernment and can quickly assess what is going on with the team of five and within the organization as a whole. They are equipped to come along side another member or rank to develop them, help to align them, and bring clarity when emotions are out of control. This serves to stabilize the group effort.

Often, the Nurturer will need someone else to dialogue with so that they do not run the risk of taking on any of the problems of the ones they are working beside. They are highly empathetic and can sympathize with others easily. When fulfilling their role, Nurturers are capable of spreading peace, joy, and harmony to everyone they meet. They can often be described as the glue that holds the effort together.

Reformers, Revelators, Proclaimers, and Educators need the support, correction and developmental support that only a Nurturer can offer. The Nurturer needs to have a Reformer that they can go to for words of direction, correction or development. Likewise, a Revelator can offer insight to the Nurturer. The Educator can support the Nurturer through knowledge. The Proclaimer can help keep a Nurturer positive by providing much needed encouragement. By working together, all of the ranks will produce a synergistic effect not available to those operating individually.

Educators

Any group undertaking needs a reliable, credible source of information as a basis upon which to make decisions. This is the role of Educators in a group. Regardless of the mountain they are working in, the task of the Educator is to seek and present information in such a way, that the group is able to grasp that knowledge and use it in their undertaking. Although the Educator is listed last in the group of five, their efforts build the foundation upon which all other activities of the group are based. Without accurate information, or the needed skills, it would be impossible for the group to succeed. Along with finding, gathering, and disseminating information, Educators will catalog and maintain that information for ease of access in future situations.

To gather the necessary information, Educators will often have an unusual ability to concentrate. They will be able to spend long periods of time researching and digging into topics. Along with the ability to concentrate, an Educator will often receive unusual insight into topics. This assists the group-of-five efforts, because it provides extra perception into the cornerstones of any project or undertaking. Accurate and valid information is the backbone of any project. It's the job of Educators to steward that information.

Within a group consisting of all five ranks, Reformers are there to see what needs to be changed and challenge the other ranks to move with them in doing it. Revelators give the up to date specifics of what needs to happen and how to achieve that. Proclaimers then get everyone on board. Nurturers take action to help everyone remain grounded as they are accomplishing the tasks they are called to do and Educators make sure that everyone knows how to do it. It is a beautiful depiction of divine teamwork in action when all five ranks are functioning in the task that they were created for.

How the Mountains Interact

At the beginning of this chapter, I promised an excursion into the world of history, to help explain God's Kingdom structure. This is where that journey begins. The purpose of the End-Times army is to take back territory that has been conceded to the enemy over generations. It is sometimes helpful to use an example taken from history in order to understand how the structure, in general, works and how that territory was lost to begin with.

When examining victories of darkness over light, there can be no clearer example than that of Hitler's rise to power and subsequent transformation of the fabric of German society from 1925 to 1945. It will serve as an unmistakable example of the process of replacing one type of ideology with another. It was possible for a small, violent group that represented a minority belief system to replace a foundation of faith, based upon hundreds of years of Christian victory represented by the legacy of Martin Luther, among others, within a span of less than 20 years.

When examining victories of light over darkness, there can be no clearer example than that of the founding of the United States of America, which was built upon the Great Awakening of 1730-1755. This awakening primarily affected people who were already Christian believers. "Sinners in the Hands of an Angry God", from Jonathan Edwards, was a key sermon generated in this movement. It stressed Hell as the reward of sinners and called for repentance from sin and a return to the principles of the Bible. Edwards ended the sermon with one final appeal, "Therefore let everyone that is out of Christ, now awake and fly from the wrath to come." It impacted an entire generation of colonists and provided the foundation for the formation of the United States of America.

General History of the Rise of the Nazi Party and Hitler – The Rise of Darkness

Many people, when confronted with the historical events that played out during the Second World War in Germany, come away with the impression that the entire nation of Germany stood behind the values and ideology of the Nazi party and of Hitler. What most people don't realize is that the NSDAP, or the Nazi party only won 2.6% of the vote, when they first attempted to influence the German government in 1928. A vast majority of the German people wanted nothing to do with them. The rise of the Nazi party actually began after the New York Stock Market Crash on October 4th, 1929. Because the German war reparations were coupled with the US dollar through the Dawes Plan, the dollar's fall caused the ensuing depression to spread to Germany as well.

The increasing difficulty with the value of the German Mark, and a difference over the budgetary plans caused the chancellor Brüning to invoke Article 48, which allowed him to create and impose laws, without the approval of the Reichstag, or parliament. This is very similar to an executive order in the USA. The failure of the economy caused the NSDAP to get 18.3% of the vote in the fall of 1930. It was now the second largest party in the Reichstag.

1932 saw two attempts, by Hitler, to gain more power and control of the German government. He stood for election for President twice and lost both times. Elections in July of 1932 saw the NSDAP rise to become the largest German party, having achieved 37.4% of the vote. This paved the way for Hitler to make a claim for the position of Chancellor. After many political maneuverings, he achieved that goal in 1933.

In a period of increasing use and abuse of Article 48, Hitler introduced censorship on January 30th, 1933, one week after having been proclaimed chancellor. With elections looming, a terrorist act against the Reichstag on February 27 left the building charred and burned. Although the attack was blamed on Communist extremists, to this day there has been debate on whether the NSDAP themselves committed the act in order to force a further shift in power.

Hitler's response to the attack was to pass an Article 48 law on the very next day, ending civil liberties in Germany. The Nazi's, who were riding high on a wave of anti-Communism, got 43.9% of the vote during the March 5th election. Their first order of business is to ban the Communist party. Using the threat of imminent danger, proven through the attack on the Reichstag, Hitler has his party pass the "Enabling Act" on March 24th, which makes him dictator for four years.

By July 14th of that same year all other political parties and trade unions have been banned and the NSDAP is left as the only legal political party in Germany. Hitler also bans strikes. He has effectively silenced any possible public opposition. In October of 1933, Hitler withdrew from the League of Nations. In this way he was able to stop outside forces from enacting sanctions or curbing his quest for power. Hitler sought to systematically silence any competing voice to his, from either within or outside of the nation.

Internal party wrangling led to Hitler having the leader of the Nazi SA group,

Röhm, executed in June of 1934. The SA's were the thug and bully group of the Nazi party, who were often sent into the streets to terrorize the citizenry into passivity. They had been attempting to join forces with the army in order to stop Hitler. On August 2nd, 1934 the Reichs-President, Paul von Hindenburg, died. Upon Hindenburg's death, Hitler combined the positions of Chancellor and President, negating any balance of power offered through the separation of those roles.

Hitler was born in Austria. He was an Austrian citizen. He had caused trouble and was thrown in jail for nine months in 1923. Had the German government made use of its authority and rights, they could have deported him and he would never have risen to power. As it was, the German government granted Hitler citizenship in 1932 and paved the way for a de-facto foreigner to take over power and lead the entire nation down a path of destruction.

One cannot help but consider how different things might have turned out, had they enforced their own laws on citizenship. Instead of standing behind their laws and the values of their nation, they caved to a passing movement forced upon the majority of the people by a small minority of the population. A laissez-faire attitude with respect to the politics of the day, a single act of carelessness led millions to suffer. Nations and cities were destroyed. Millions were killed. Countless others were left homeless and destitute.

In order to explain the Kingdom principles from a negative perspective, I have given you the background timeline of events leading to the rise of Hitler in Nazi Germany. Now it is possible to explain the actions of the Nazis in each of the mountains or spheres of influence. These actions helped to usurp the Christian heritage and tradition of Germany and replaced it with an ideology of hate and violence within a very short period of time.

General History of the Founding of the United States of America – The Rise of Light

Pilgrims first populated the American Colonies. Contrary to what is popularly believed; those Pilgrims did not choose to flee Europe in order to obtain religious freedom. The usual story claims that they were fleeing from persecution ordered by England's King James. The reality was that the Pilgrims had lived in Leiden in the Dutch Republic for many years. There, they were able to practice their religion without persecution of any type.

The question then becomes, why did the Pilgrims choose to leave their safe home to make the long and difficult journey to a new and dangerous land? The answer can be found in a document called the Mayflower Compact. It was the first governing document of the Plymouth Colony. Written by the male passengers of the Mayflower, it was signed by the 41 male passengers of the Mayflower on November 11, 1620 (Julian Calendar). There were a total of 102 people on board.

The text of the Compact, in modern English, reads:
> *...Having undertaken, for the Glory of God, and advancements of the Christian faith and honor of our King and Country, a voyage to plant the first colony in the Northern parts of Virginia, do by these presents, solemnly and mutually, in the presence of God, and one another, covenant and combine ourselves together into a civil body politic; for our better ordering, and preservation and furtherance of the ends aforesaid; and by virtue hereof to enact, constitute, and frame, such just and equal laws, ordinances, acts, constitutions, and offices, from time to time, as shall be thought most meet and convenient for the general good of the colony; unto which we promise all due submission and obedience.*[1]

The Pilgrims undertook the long journey across a deadly ocean in order to spread the Christian faith to a new colony. They were missionaries. After eighteen years of difficult labor, the colonies had been established to such an extent, that a more structured form of governmental law was needed. The Fundamental Orders of Connecticut, written in 1639, was the result.

This document makes it very clear that the fundamental driving ideology of the colonists was a belief in an Almighty God and in the necessity for submission to His will. Here is a quote.
> *For as much as it hath pleased Almighty God by the wise disposition of his divine providence so to order and dispose of things that we the Inhabitants and Residents of Windsor, Hartford and Wethersfield are now cohabiting and dwelling in and upon the River of Connectecotte and the lands thereunto adjoining;*

*and well knowing where a people are gathered together the word of
God requires that to maintain the peace and union of such a people
there should be an orderly and decent Government established
according to God, …;*

*and do for ourselves and our successors and such as shall be adjoined
to us at any time hereafter, enter into Combination and Confederation
together,* ***to maintain and preserve the liberty and purity of the
Gospel of our Lord Jesus which we now profess (emphasis added)****, as
also, the discipline of the Churches, which according to the truth of the
said Gospel is now practiced amongst us;*

*as also in our civil affairs to be guided and governed according to
such Laws, Rules, Orders and Decrees as shall be made, ordered, and
decreed as followeth:*[2]

The Fundamental Orders of Connecticut, which was passed into law on
January 14th, 1639 made it abundantly clear what the motivating factor of the
colonists was. The law and structure of government was created and set up in
order to "maintain the peace and union of the people", because "the word of
God requires that" and that there should be an "orderly and decent
Government established according to God". The ultimate driving force,
however, was "to maintain and preserve the liberty and purity of the Gospel
of our Lord Jesus, which we now profess".

The colonists were Christians who had subjected every aspect of their lives
to God. After the initial period of colonization and of establishment of the
foundational governmental structures, secularism began to gain in
momentum. A short search of websites will provide many online discourses
claiming that all of the Founding Fathers of the nation were without religion
of any type and did not believe in Jesus Christ. Although there was a time
period in the late 1600's and early 1700's in which the colonists, in general,
became lukewarm in their enthusiasm for the Gospel, this changed with the
advent of a monumental move of God that impacted the entire East Coast.

In the time period from 1730 to 1760, the American Colonies experienced
The First Great Awakening. This was a revival and awakening movement led
by a group of prominent preachers. Two of these clergy were from the

colonies; the other was a traveling preacher visiting the colonies from England. Founded upon a strong message of repentance, redemption, and a return to moral principles based upon Biblical values, this movement laid the foundation for the rebellion against the oppressive British regime. This revolt eventually became the American Revolution.

Colonial American's understanding of God, of religion, of the world around them, and of themselves changed drastically as a result of the First Great Awakening. Even those who, like Benjamin Franklin, were neither of the clergy nor especially religious in the traditional sense of the word, had enough respect for the movement, that they supported it in any way that they were able to.

Franklin, a signer of the Declaration of Independence and a leading figure in the new government was a great admirer of George Whitefield and used his paper, The Gazette, to inform the public about the awakening. In fact, Franklin printed Whitefield's sermons on the front page. During the time of the awakening, he published all of Whitefield's sermons and journals. Franklin used the power of the media to spread the foundational values of the soon to be United States of America.

Throughout the Revolution, which began in 1765, the clergy played a vital role in encouraging the colonists to stand for Biblical values above the laws imposed by the British Empire. Dubbed the "Black Robe Regiment" these preachers often led militias of church members during skirmishes against the Redcoats of the British army. Their fiery sermons and their steadfastness in the face of the enemy earned them their enemy's respect.

After the war was over, the business of creating a legal basis for the new nation's government began. Many of the Founding Fathers had been notably impacted during the First Great Awakening. Many others had, themselves, been preachers during the movement. Of the 204 men, who can be considered as one of the Founding Fathers, 100% of them logged their affiliation with Christian theology. Of those Christians, 54.7% of them were Anglican/Episcopalian, 18.6% were Presbyterian, and 16.8% considered themselves Congregationalists.[3] Of those that signed the Declaration of Independence, four had been full-time preachers or clergymen during the awakening. Many more of them were sons of clergymen.

There is a movement today to cut ties with the USA's foundational history. The 1619 project of the New York Times Magazine seeks to remove the actual Judeo-Christian founded history of the United States and to replace it with a contrived narrative designed to destroy the very fabric of the nation. According to their mission statement, the project "aims to reframe the country's history…"[4] Fortunately, a host of prominent historians have vocally denounced the perversion of historical fact.[5] A struggle has begun between the opposing viewpoints. In an effort to appear "progressive" many schools have adopted the 1619 project and have failed to place the tenants of that work within the context of documented history. It remains to be seen how long this struggle will continue and which side will ultimately succeed.

The blatant attempt to reshape history in the USA is not restricted to the 1619 project. In addition to that movement there are others who claim that the primary documents, which influenced the Founding Fathers in the creation of the three major governmental documents, were purely secular in nature. By negating the influence of Judeo-Christian values on the creation of the founding documents, they seek to advance the ideology of secular humanism within the nation. This premise is negated by the fact that although most of the Founding Fathers were well read and familiar with a great number of secular texts, the fundamental work influencing their lives was the Bible. Their contact with the First Great Awakening and their backgrounds made that inevitable and the values and ideals imbedded into the fledgling nation's foundational documents created paid homage to that.

The Kingdom Mountain

Purpose:

- To come alongside initiatives in the other mountains and assist them in their efforts.
- To create initiatives, which connect smaller efforts in various mountains together.
- To give direction, guidance and encourage initiatives from a higher vantage point.
- To remain in constant communication with The Holy Spirit, receiving

orders to do what is necessary to advance the Kingdom.

- To be the command center for the battle to influence culture.

The Kingdom Mountain is the command central in the battle to implement an ideological shift in society. It has the highest place among the mountains, not because it is better, but simply because it has a better vantage point. People working out of this mountain have the job of coordinating and creating efforts that involve multiple mountains. This creates a synergy, which will help the universal effort achieve more, than the individual mountains could do on their own.

Darkness

Hitler was very methodical in choosing his inner circle of leaders. But, as is common with most despots, he refused to delegate and entrust power to those in command of other areas. This caused wrangling and confusion among the leadership and was the cause of great losses in battle and the ultimate failure of the government. It is, indeed, possible to obtain power and misuse that power to mold a society into a form and push it into a position not intended by The Creator. It will, however, not be possible for anyone to make it stay in that position for any great length of time.

Light

A group of profoundly intelligent and ethically minded men came together in 1776 to sign the document, which would separate the American colonies from England and allow the creation of a singularly unique form of government. These men were as diverse as any group of men could be and represented a full spectrum of different occupations and religious practices. Of the fifty-six men signing the Declaration of Independence, two of them were full-time ministers; two others had been trained as full-time ministers. A whole slew of them were the sons of clergymen.

One of the most amazing things about this group of leaders was the fact that every single one of them served in multiple roles during the span of their lives. It can, with a great deal of certainty, be said that these men were all working out of the Kingdom Mountain. As Kingdom Mountain people, they moved from one sphere of influence to the other, as their skills were needed. For example: if you examine the person of Thomas Jefferson, you will discover a person who was the chief author of the Declaration of Independence; a member of the Virginia House of Delegates; the Governor of Virginia; the Associate Envoy to France; the Minister to the French Court; the United States Secretary of State; the Vice-President; the President of the United States; and ultimately, the chief founder of the University of Virginia in 1810. The caliber of people called to the Kingdom Mountain during the period of revolution in American History was on par with the level of advancements that the newly formed United States of America experienced.

The Church Mountain

Purpose:

- To be the source of a group's or nation's values, behaviors, language, and rituals.
- To establish the model of appropriate behavior for the culture.
- To use the chosen values, behaviors, language, and rituals to create the framework for the fabric of the entire society and culture.
- To establish the principles, which will provide the greatest quality of life and highest level of prosperity for the members of the community.
- To be the point of reference on questions of values, behaviors, language, and rituals in a culture and society.

The purpose of the Church Mountain is to be the source of all values, behaviors, rituals and language used in a nation. It is the highest of the mountains that are under the Kingdom Mountain. Because it has the highest position, it must fulfill its mandate in order to influence the other mountains. It has the highest position of authority and this position cannot be left vacant. If the leadership of the mountain is weak and unable or unwilling to defend its position against other outside forces, this will cause a power vacuum. The Church will essentially abdicate the authority given to it and another ideology will replace it.

Darkness

The Nazi party, or the demonic forces advancing the goals of the party, recognized the essential role of the Church in shaping and forming society.

Soon after having been declared Dictator, on September 27th, 1933, Hitler named Ludwig Müller as the only "Reichsbischof" (State Bishop) of the Lutheran Church in Germany. Müller's assignment was to unify the church and bring it into alignment with the ideology of the Nazi party. He failed miserably at the task given to him. This was due to tremendous resistance generated by the "Bekennenden Kirche". The "Bekennenden Kirche" was an organization of animated Christians, who came together on May 29th, 1934 in defiance of the push by the Nazi party to completely take over the Church and to use its power to dominate. Müller was relieved of his duties in September of 1935. He remained "Reichsbischof" in name only. The Lutheran Church was then placed under the authority of the Minister for Church Affairs. It was also subject to the "Reichskirchenausschuss" or State Church Committee. Hitler had removed the autonomy of the church and placed it under direct control of the Nazi party.

Most people are aware of the Nazi party's push to persecute, hunt down, and exterminate all Jews within Germany and the territories that it conquered. What most people are not aware of is that the Nazi party began a merciless campaign to shut out and to shut down all competing ideologies almost from the first moment that it had the power to do so. Its primary weapon to do this was concentration camps. Throughout the entire time of Nazi domination of Germany, its objective was to remove ALL people from society that could be a threat to the success and advancement of the Nazi ideology. This included prominent critics of the system from within the Church. One of the most well known of these critics was Dietrich Bonhoeffer. Bonhoeffer was a Lutheran theologian and a vocal critic of the NSDAP.

He was a very outspoken representative of the "Bekennenden Kirche" and of the tenants of that group. He was also a member of the German Resistance. In April 1933, he embarked upon a course of open criticism of the Nazi's systematic persecution of the Jews. He also led the fight against the "Deutsche Christen", which was the Nazi institution created to represent the church in Germany. As part of his work in the "Bekennenden Kirche", he was named director of the seminary in 1935. This seminary taught Biblical Christian values and existed until 1940, when it was declared illegal and was disbanded. In 1940, the Nazi party banned him from openly preaching or speaking in front of a public of any type. In 1941, the ban was enlarged to include any and all written publications. All efforts undertaken by the Nazi party to shut this very vocal Christian down were futile. So, in April of 1943, they arrested him. During his time in a prison in Berlin, he wrote many letters, which his friend collected and published after his death as a book entitled *Widerstand und Ergebung*.

In the Spring of 1945, Bonhoeffer was moved from his prison in Berlin to a concentration camp in Flossenbürg, Bavaria. The war was drawing to a close and the gunfire of American troops could be heard advancing on the camp. On April 9th, shortly before the American army freed the Flossenbürg concentration camp on the 23rd of April, Hitler personally gave orders that Bonheoffer was to be executed. Hitler committed suicide seven days later. Bonhoeffer's story is only one of the many, which occurred in Germany during the NSDAP period. The Nazi party understood the prominent position that the Church had in influencing culture. And they used every imaginable method to ensure that their ideology was the only one in the country.

Light

The First Great Awakening of 1730-1755 provided the basis upon which the values of the United States, anchored in the Declaration of Independence (1776), the Articles of Confederation (drafted 1777, ratified 1781) and the Constitution of the United States of America (1789), were established. In an environment that was staunchly and conservatively religious, three men stepped into the forefront and changed the face of church life in New England during this time. These men were: Jonathan Edwards, George Whitefield, and Samuel Davies. The main message of their sermons was a personal relationship with God and a return to Biblical principles of conduct and morality.

Jonathan Edwards preached primarily about sin, Hell and the need of every man for a savior. The goal of his sermons was to bring conviction to each person, whether a believer or not, and to cause them to humble themselves and return to their Savior. It was only through the process of personal conviction, Edwards believed, that people could be brought into right standing with their Creator. He placed great emphasis on the power of a personal religious experience and greatly distrusted religious leadership. Edwards taught that the only valid religious experience was an intensely personal one. The tools of ritual, tradition, ceremony, sacramentalism, and hierarchy, which were taught by the religious elite of the day, were tools used by the religious leaders to draw people to themselves, but not to their God. Edwards' background stemmed from the Puritan and Calvinist churches. His sermons deviated greatly from those root beliefs.

Building upon the fire bed of sermons preached in New England in the early years of the Awakening, an Anglican preacher, visiting the colonies from England, lit the match and ignited the tinder already laid. George Whitefield, an itinerant minister, traveled the length and breadth of the colonies for two years from 1739-1740, drawing large crowds in open-air events and led countless people to salvation through repentance.

Edwards built a fire with his exhortation of Hell as the just place of habitation for sinners. Whitefield, on the other hand, taught about a merciful God. According to Whitefield, people were not predestined to Hell and damnation. Instead, each man or woman could choose where he or she was to spend eternity. Whitefield was a very passionate and enthusiastic preacher. His charisma and his preaching skills drew large crowds of people to hear his sermons. Because of this, the First Great Awakening became a great social event, influencing many people in New England at the time. His sermons and journals were published on the front page of Benjamin Franklin's gazette, which added even more fuel to the revival fire.

Samuel Davies, a Presbyterian minister, also traveled the length and breadth of the colonies preaching. Davies, as did Edwards and Whitefield, preached a message of redemption from sin through repentance and acceptance of Jesus Christ as savior. His audience, however, was the slaves. In his sermons, he preached that all men could equally attain salvation and enter into the Promised Land. The color of skin and social status could not hinder the redemptive gift given by Jesus Christ. He was credited for converting large numbers of African slaves to Christianity and taught that it was the duty of slaveholders to provide adequate instruction and education to slaves, so that they could use those literacy skills to better understand Biblical values and tenants.

These men built the foundation for the First Great Awakening in Colonial America. In the years that followed, however, it was the average pulpit preacher preaching sermons in local churches throughout the colonies, who hammered these values home. This "Black-Robe Regiment" was feared by the British and ultimately credited as being the true cause of the victory of the colonists against The British Empire. The broad-based revival and return to Biblical principles and values set the stage for the founding of the United States of America. Because of the First Great Awakening, people were made familiar with sin and with the need for repentance. Following that, they were given the opportunity to begin a new way of life through the redemptive work of Jesus Christ on the Cross. It also encouraged a life of continued self-examination with a subsequent commitment to personal morality based upon the values contained in the Bible.

Without a foundation built upon a thorough knowledge and belief in Biblical principles, the application of the Kingdom structure could not have succeeded in Colonial America. The great men, who made up the Kingdom level of God's Kingdom structure had all been part of, or, at some level, had been greatly impacted by the First Great Awakening. The Bible provided the values and the ideology that was then implemented in all of the spheres of influence in the newly created United States of America. And, although overt references to Christianity are not found in these documents, the values are most definitely included in them.

The Family Mountain

Purpose:

- To serve members of a social grouping by helping them to grow, mature, and become the best version of themselves that they can be.
- To nurture members into implementing the values, behaviors, language and rituals of society.
- To use the established strength of the family unit to move out into the wider community and serve where there is need.
- To create a set of values and behaviors for the intimate family unit.
- To ensure the continuation of the family unit and of the wider society at the same time by creating whole, healthy, functioning and socialized individuals.

The primary function of the Family Mountain is to ensure the continuation of a society by making sure that each individual member of that society is healthy, healed, whole and socialized in the culture, norms and mores of that societal structure. Families instill values. In the Kingdom structure, the Church provides those values. If the Church is too weak, unable to, or refuses to provide the foundational values, another entity will fill that role and provide them for society.

Darkness

This is what happened during the NSDAP time in German history. Since secular humanism was widely accepted and promoted at that time, the Nazi's were able to infiltrate society and promote their values in every arena of society. They were also able to do this within the sphere of the family. Hitler's plan was to dominate the entire European continent. In order to achieve this goal, he needed soldiers. Actually, he needed many loyal soldiers. Therefore, the NSDAP family policy was to establish many incentives designed to convince German families to have great numbers of children. Not just any children, but children that would be healthy, strong, and have the "right" genetic make-up.

On July 14th, 1933, a few months after Hitler had been declared dictator for four years, the "Gesetz zur Verhuetung erbkranken Nachwuchses" was passed into law. Translated, this was the "Law to Protect Against Genetically Ill Offspring". It was put into force on the same day that the Nazi party banned all other political parties, trade unions, and strikes. The purpose of this law was to protect the genetic make up of the "Arian" race and permitted the forcible sterilization of people who were assumed to be carrying deficient genetic material. The sterilizations could be enforced on both men and women, even against their will.

Two years and two months later, the NSDAP passed another series of laws affecting families during their party conference in Nuernburg. These laws were collectively known as the "Nuernberger Gesetze" or the "Nuernberger Rassegesetze". Two separate types of laws were contained in the package. The first of these dealt with the issue of nationality and who was considered a true citizen of the Third Reich. It was the law that determined what level of citizenship you had based upon the degree of relation that you had with Jews.

The second type of law passed at the NSDAP conference was a law that sought to protect the "German blood". Effectively, it forbade marriages between Jews and non-Jews. The first of the two types of laws passed on that day was the determining factor in establishing the level of Jewishness a person had. Based upon that determination, a person was either allowed to marry another person or not. Not only was it forbidden for a "German" to marry a Jew, in the second paragraph of that law, "mixed" couples were forbidden to have intercourse. In addition to those two laws, a third law was also passed the "Erbgesundheitsgesetz" sought to protect the "German blood" from degradation through genetic illnesses and through illnesses carried by the individuals seeking to get married. Before they got married, each partner was required to get a "report card" which provided documentation to the person issuing the marriage license that the partners were not carrying communicable or genetic diseases.

After it was determined that a couple was healthy and able to produce strong, healthy, and non-Jewish offspring, the Nazi party sought to give all types of incentives for those couples to produce lots and lots of them. It invented the "Mother Cross", which was a medal, in the shape of a cross with the Nazi emblem at the center that was given to women based upon the number of children that they bore. A bronze cross was given to a mother who had four or five children, a silver cross was given for six or seven children, and women who had had eight children with "clean" blood earned the gold cross.

The role of couples during the Nazi era was to produce as many genetically and racially perfect children as possible. These children were then groomed for their prescribed roles within the Nazi societal structure. But the grooming of the children was not left up to the parents. Instead, beginning at age of six or seven, when the children were required to start going to school, the Nazi party took over their socialization.

Light

Families, in the era of the Revolution were modeled upon what we would call "traditional" roles. Women were responsible for managing the household and the men were the ones that were going out to fight. But it was during the most divisive times of war that these "set in stone" functions began to shift. The Homespun Movement began as part of the anti-British effort. In order to reduce the amount of imported British clothing or materials, Patriot women spun their own thread and made their own cloth. This provided the necessary raw material to produce clothing and helped to support the boycott of British textiles. In addition to providing cloth and clothing for their own families, these women made additional cloth to produce clothing and blankets for the Continental Army.

Along with their service to the Homespun movement, Patriot women also proved to be an invaluable asset to the cause for independence. This occurred, in part, by radically boycotting all manufactured goods imported from Britain. In an appeal to the women of South Carolina, Christopher Gadsden explained, "Our political salvation, as this crisis, depends altogether upon the strictest economy, that the women could, with propriety, have the principal management thereof..."[6] It was through self-sacrifice and self-discipline, both Biblical characteristics, that the Patriot women were able to support the advancement of the revolutionary cause. Most historic sources of the time show that only about a third of the colonist were Patriots and supported the anti-British effort. An additional third were pro-British "Tories". The last third of the population were people who bounced back and forth between the two sides waiting to see which one came out on top. Many rural communities were uninvolved and neutral, but because of the steadfastness of the boycott and of the Patriot women, they were brought "into the growing community of resistance".[7]

The Boston Tea Party, which took place in 1773 in Boston, Massachusetts, was the most well known of the boycott events. It sparked other initiatives. Among these was the Edenton Tea Party, a political protest started in Edenton, North Carolina. Where the Boston Tea Party was a protest led by the Patriot men, the Edenton Tea Party was a protest of fifty-one women, led by Penelope Barker. In a statement signed on October 25th, 1774, they vowed to give up tea and boycott other British products. The motivation for becoming involved was to resist, "until such time as all acts which tend to enslave our Native country shall be repealed."[8]

On the other end of the colonies, in Philadelphia, the Ladies Association got together to collect funds for the war effort. This encouraged other states to follow suit. The wife of the Pennsylvania governor Joseph Reed, Esther de Berdt Reed, founded the first chapter of the association. Together with the daughter of Benjamin Franklin, Sarah Franklin Bache, they were very successful in spreading the message and raising sorely needed funds. The various organizations run by women in the colonies were able to raise over $300,000.[9]

But Patriot women weren't just making cloth, being frugal, gathering money and offering their homes to various war efforts. They also fought in the war next to their men. Some of them did it because they were unable to get along financially without their men, others joined because they were afraid of what an advancing British army would do to a solitary woman. Known as camp followers, they served the army by cleaning, cooking, nursing, sewing, and by scavenging for supplies. Some estimates claim that 20,000 women belonged to the Continental Army; others state that the number made up about 3% of the army.

Some women, upon the death of their spouse, chose to enlist as a fighting force in the Continental Army. These battle soldiers were greatly respected by the enlisted men. The other women, who joined because of the enlistment bounty, were greatly disliked. Certain key figures in the war were able to conceal their identity and fight alongside the men as equals, still others were able to work for the war effort as spies.[10] Generally speaking, therefore, women during the Revolutionary War had many vital roles to play in support of the war effort (Galatians 3:28).

The Education Mountain

Purpose:

- To develop and perfect the means and methodology for transferring acquired skills, knowledge and values from one individual to another.
- To foster research into the field of cognitive learning.
- To develop and perfect existing educational tools.
- To search for other means in order to enhance and improve the learning experience.
- To encourage participation in continued learning regardless of age or level of ability.

The Education Mountain is the next most influential societal sphere, after the Family Mountain. It is in this mountain, that people are taught the chosen ideology of society. The cultural norms do not originate in this mountain. Instead, in the best case, the values are produced in the Church Mountain and stem from a religious code of ethics and morals. In the worst case, they can originate in any of the other mountains, essentially from a human source, if the church abdicates its authority and is too weak to provide or defend them.

Darkness

Beginning at age six or seven, children in Nazi Germany were taken away from the nurturing environment of their family homes and placed into schools, where they could be indoctrinated into the NSDAP ideology. In order to ensure the purity of the transference of those values, the NSDAP vetted each teacher and removed any teacher teaching values that were contrary to the party ideology. Students were urged to report any teacher activity that was against party lines. As a result, 97% of the teachers in Germany during the Nazi era were members of the Nazi Teacher's Association.

Students were encouraged to attend classes during school holidays. This provided the Nazi party with yet another opportunity to influence and indoctrinate children, as the party developed the curriculum for these "holiday sessions". The children were being molded at a young age to adopt the morals, values, and viewpoint of the NSDAP. At about the age of eleven, children began a more intensive study of the dominant political viewpoint of the day. This occurred through an institution known as the "Hitlerjugend" or "Hitler Youth". Because of the different roles designated for each sex by the NSDAP, the children were strictly divided into organizations designed for either the girls, or the boys.

Girls were sent into the "Jungmaedelbund", the association for young girls. In this association, they were taught the history of the NSDAP, the Hitler Youth and of Adolf Hitler. They were required to participate in sports and were drilled in discipline and submission. This was done so that they would develop a feeling of solidarity with the government and the German citizenry. When they had reached the age of 18, young women were then sent to "Bund Deutscher Maedel" or BDM, which was an organization designed to prepare young women for their designated role in Nazi society. The institution was dubbed "Bald Deutsche Mutter", by the citizenry. Translated as "Soon to be a German Mother", this nomenclature accurately, albeit sarcastically, described the purpose of the association.

In this organization, they were taught the skills that they would need to become strong and brave German woman who were capable of running a household, being a mother and raising many, many children. In addition to being instructed on those "life skills", young German women were taught to recognize skills and qualities, genetic and otherwise, in a potential mate. Sports provided the opportunity to build strength in the women and prepare them for childbirth. The additional training received in the area of "Glaube und Schoenheit" or "Faith and Beauty" prepared them to be the perfect physical embodiment of the ideal Nazi mother. In this training course, they were taught about hygiene, sports and household management. It was the last stop before they were required to spend a year receiving practical training in a household or in an agricultural setting.

Boys, on the other hand, joined the "Jungvolk" or the "Young Citizens" at the age of ten. Similar to the girls, the young boys in Nazi Germany learned about the history of the NSDAP, the Hitler Youth and of Adolf Hitler. In contrast to the girls, they also took part in target practice exercises using an air gun. These drills were designed to awaken their interest in the things of war. This was the first step towards becoming a soldier in Hitler's army, since Hitler envisioned European domination as his ultimate plan for the people of Germany.

When they reached the age of 14, the young men were sent to the "Hitlerjugend" or "Hitler Youth". The primary purpose of HJ was to coach young men for their future role as soldiers in Hitler's army. In addition to sport training to prepare them for the physical challenges, they also were instructed in the daily routine facing a soldier. In paramilitary exercises, the young men were drilled and prepared to become strong, well-trained, fearless soldiers that unequivocally supported their Fatherland and their "Fuehrer".

During the Nazi era, the entire school curriculum was altered to indoctrinate young children into the ideology of the Nazi party. In order to achieve that goal, the NSDAP changed the school plan and the contents of the individual school subjects. The extent to which the content was manipulated depended upon the subject matter and how that could be biased to reflect their ideology. Of primary interest to the NSDAP were the subjects of Sports, History, and German. Because of this, these subjects were given more hours within the school plan. An increase in sports hours led to stronger and healthier bodies. Increasing the focus on history allowed the party to highlight the glory of the German nation and its people. Spending more time in a classroom studying German opened the German language, German literature and German culture to be used by the party to propagate its ideology.

The subject of Biology allowed the Nazi idea of "racial purity" and "racial superiority" to be taught at a young age. Children were taught about genetics and the problems of heredity. Geography offered an opportunity to teach about the original expanse of the country of Germany and how the Versailles Treaty caused a loss of German territory. All forms of science were used to teach about the potential for military application of scientific knowledge. Students were taught the physics behind ballistics and shooting. They were instructed in civil engineering, with a view towards road and bridge construction. Chemistry was used to instruct on the effects of poisonous gasses on the human body.

Light

> *"I know no safe depositary of the ultimate powers of the society but the people themselves; and if we think them not enlightened enough to exercise their control with a wholesome discretion, the remedy is not to take it from them, but to inform their discretion by education. This is the true corrective of abuses of constitutional power." Thomas Jefferson to William C. Jarvis, 1820*

Education in the colonies began with schoolbooks brought over from England. The primary textbook was the *English Protestant Tutor*. The tutors were transported to the colonies for many years. When the printer, Benjamin Harris, who had been printing them in England, fled the Catholic ascendancy under James II in 1686, he took the publication rights with him. Then he began printing the book in the colonies. Harris changed the name of the textbook to *The New England Primer* and added additional materials that made it very popular in colonial schools. First published between 1687 and 1690, it remained the main schoolbook in the colonies until Noah Webster's *Blue Back Speller* slowly began to replace it after 1790. As such, it remained in print until well into the 19th century. In some schools it was even still in use in the early 20th century.

There were many versions of the Primer printed over the time period that it was in use. Its major content included all or some of the following: the alphabet, vowels, consonants, double letters and syllabariums of two letters to six letter syllables. In order to teach this material, the Primer used alphabetical assistants, religious maxims, woodcuts, moral lessons, acronyms, and catechism answers.[11] The prime underlying ideology was the Word of God. The Bible offered numerous ways in which to teach the lessons contained in the textbook. The Word was such an important part of the text, that it became known locally as "The Little Bible of New England". The work was about 90 pages in length.

During the First Great Awakening, a number of changes were made to the Primer. The primary message before that time had been the damnation of man because of sin. The message that was preached during the Awakening shifted from the damnation of man because of sin to the love of God displayed through the sacrifice of His only Son Jesus in place of the sinner. In order to reflect this change in theology, some of the content was altered. The couplet for the letter C was altered from "The cat does play/And after slay" to the more faith-based "Christ crucify'd/For sinners dy'd". In addition to direct changes in the content, additional faith-based literature was added to the Primer such as prayers and hymns. Some versions included The Lord's Prayer, the Apostles' Creed, the Ten Commandments, "Cradle Hymn", by Isaac Watts[12], among others.

What most people are unaware of is, that when they teach their child the nighttime prayer,
> *"Now I lay me down to sleep,*
> *I pray the Lord my soul to keep,*
> *If I should die before I awake,*
> *I pray the Lord my soul to take."*[13]

they are actually reciting a passage from the 1750 edition of The New

England Primer. This pilgrim and colonist textbook worked its way so deeply into the American culture, that parts of it are still as active today, as they were over 250 years ago. The New England Primer laid the foundation for the morals and values of many generations of colonist children. Building on this foundation, the next generation started a push to found schools of higher learning.

Of the eight Ivy League universities, and of the nine institutions of higher learning that pre-date the American Revolution, seven of them have religious mottos. Of those seven universities, five of them were founded by a religious synod or by clergymen. All of them offered theology as a field of study. Samuel Davies, the famous Presbyterian minister closely associated with the Great Awakening ultimately became the fourth president of Princeton University, one of those eight Ivy League Universities. Princeton was an institution that had been founded by the Calvinists- Presbyterians.

The American Revolution brought with it a group of stellar men and women who, among other things, greatly affected the direction of education within the newly formed United States of America. Among these great patriots were: John Witherspoon, the only active clergyman among the signers of the Declaration of Independence became the president of the College of New Jersey, which later became Princeton University from 1768-1792, after having served in various positions within the government. George Walton, another signer of the Declaration of Independence, also began his service for the newly formed country by holding various positions in the government. Being self-taught, education was never far from his mind. He was the founder of the Richmond Academy and Franklin College, which later became the University of Georgia. Benjamin Rush, a doctor who also held numerous political positions, among them the position of Surgeon General in the Middle Department of the Continental Army in 1777, was an instructor and physician at the University of Pennsylvania in 1778, and professor of Medical Theory and Clinical Practice at the University of Pennsylvania from 1791-1813.

Although Judith Sargent Murray was never an educator or held an administrative role in an educational institution, she was one of the most influential educational voices of her time. From 1784 until her death in 1820, she wrote and published hundreds of works ranging from magazine articles on the role of the female in society to poetry, plays, essays and a regularly appearing paper column written under a pseudonym. The publication of her letters has reached 10 volumes and includes letters written to many greats of the American Revolution such as George Washington.

Called the "Father of American Scholarship and Education", Noah Webster was a university student during the War for Independence. After writing a series of newspaper articles, he founded a private elementary school, where his "blue-backed" speller and other books were developed, which educated five generations of students. He later went on to write "An American Dictionary of the English Language" in 1828. He later said,

> *"The moral principles and precepts contained in the scriptures ought to form the basis of all our civil constitutions and laws. All the miseries and evils which men suffer from vice, crime, ambition, injustice, oppression, slavery, and war, proceed from their despising or neglecting the precepts contained in the Bible."*

The Government Mountain

Purpose:

- To implement a chosen set of values.
- To apply and enforce the chosen ideals at all levels and in all spheres of society.
- To defend the belief system against outside competing interests.
- To defend the chosen principles against forces opposing it from within.
- To create and maintain a system of justice to determine compliance with or infraction against the chosen set of values.

As with all of the mountains or spheres of influence, the Government Mountain is a neutral entity. Its purpose is to implement a chosen set of principles on the widest possible scale within a society. When operating within that purpose, it is irrelevant which form of government is used to apply and enforce those values. It also makes no difference, which set of ideals is chosen by a society as the purpose and function of this sphere of influence will remain the same.

There can, however, be a large difference in the effects of the implementation of those tenets on society. This difference will depend upon the source from which those ideals are taken. In the best case, the values will be generated from within the Church Mountain. In an even more ideal situation, they will be ones that bring and create the highest level of quality of life for people within the society. Generated from another mountain or from within the Government mountain itself, those beliefs can end up causing great damage to the citizenry.

Darkness

The time period of NSDAP domination in the German nation offers both the best-case and worst-case example of taking dominion over a sphere of influence. It is the best-case example, because of the near perfection in implementing the chosen value system in all other mountains. It is the worst-case example, because those values were generated from within the Government Mountain, itself. The danger of implementing a belief system generated from within the Government Mountain lies in the complete lack of balance of power. Instead of a system of principles being neutral and the government taking that belief system and applying it to all aspects of society, the government **becomes** the source of those values. This is a recipe for disaster.

The NSDAP set the value system in Germany at that time. It also did everything in its power to shut down all competing ideologies. The first step was to systematically ban all other political parties and centralize power. This began in 1933 by declaring other political parties illegal. It continued with the removal of state level representation. By 1935, Hitler had managed to completely take away the right of citizens to determine their own representation. Local mayors and city council members were appointed by the ministry of the interior, the citizens of a town or city no longer elected them. It dictated all aspects of the citizen's private life, including the most intimate properties by designating who was able to marry and who could have children. In doing so it also created a two-tier society in which there were full citizens and others, like the Jews, who were not. Along with the degradation of certain citizens, it began a course to remove all other competing ideologies. Primarily this was directed toward the Jewish religion, which had strong traditions and beliefs that could not be made compatible with the NSDAP ideology. It continued by persecuting Christian religious leaders who were critical of the system.

Within families, the NSDAP sought to usurp the natural authoritative function of parents. By bringing children into an environment, where they were force-fed Nazi ideology at a young age, the party worked to drive a wedge between children and parents. Ultimately, children were encouraged by the system to "tell-on" their parents, if these engaged in activities or expressed opinions, which were counter to Nazi ideology. Children of parents found to hold sympathies with anti-Nazi groupings were forcibly removed from their homes and brought into other homes where they would be raised in an environment that supported the NSDAP agenda. In many cases, the children of dissidents were given up for adoption by the State. Some of these children never saw their parents again.

It removed teachers with opposing viewpoints and altered school curriculum. By setting up a teaching program designed to indoctrinate children into the ideology of the Nazi party even from the youngest age, the NSDAP was able to alter thought processes and create manipulated and brainwashed citizens loyal to the country and its leader. The program continued with the older children, who were trained to fulfill the only two possible roles in society: that of a mother, and that of a soldier.

It removed the right of citizens to self-government by moving power away from the locality to the central government. In 1933 the NSDAP under Hitler removed power from the state governmental structure and transferred that power to the national government. By 1935, they had managed to change the election laws so that local communities no longer had the right to elect officials. Cities and villages were not allowed to vote for a mayor or city council member, as that system of governance had been altered. Local representation was provided through appointment decided upon at the Ministry of the Interior. It infiltrated every media avenue and created a system of propaganda in order to alter the thought processes and values of its citizens. It set up a system so that people were encouraged to spy on their neighbors, friends, or even family members and to report their activities to the party, when those ran counter to the party ideology and goals. Many dissidents and members of the anti-Nazi resistance lost their lives in concentration camps as the result of this.

The Nazi party and Hitler did not stop until their dogma was the only pattern of thought allowed in people's heads. People living in Germany at the time had no options and no choice. They were not followers because they necessarily believed in the tenants of the system. They were followers, for the most part, because they had been forced and manipulated into becoming that. This is usually the result, when a governmental ideology usurps the position reserved for the Church Mountain. The penalties for doing this are suffering, war, and poverty. Sometimes, this effect lasts over many, many generations.

Light

In stark contrast to the centralization of power exhibited through the NSDAP in Germany, the fledgling United States government sought in every imaginable way, to move the seat of power away from the central governmental structure and into the hands of ordinary citizens. The first instance of this was very significantly stated in the first document issued by the young political authority.

Within the Declaration of Independence, the staunch Patriots stated that, "We hold these truths to be self-evident, that all men are created equal, that they are endowed by their Creator with unalienable Rights, that among these are Life, Liberty and the pursuit of Happiness. That to secure these rights, Governments are instituted among Men, deriving their just powers from the consent of the governed."[14] The Declaration then goes on to list the eighteen grievances of the 13 original States of the United States towards the King of England. Of these objections, the bulk of them dealt with issues of the distribution of power and the misuse of power with respect to governance.

The Declaration made the source of its inspiration plain to see and easy to recognize for everyone. The document was less of a political statement as it was a declaration of allegiance to the governing principles upon which the nation would be founded. The thirteen states aligned themselves to higher principles and "unalienable Rights" given to them by a "Creator" and not magnanimously bestowed upon them by a government.

That particular passage of the Declaration of Independence ultimately became the sentence in the English language to represent the moral standard of the United States of America. Abraham Lincoln, one of the most important and influential Presidents in the history of the nation, built his political philosophy upon the foundation of the Declaration. He often argued, that the Declaration was the statement of principles through which the United States Constitution needed to be interpreted.[15] The Declaration of Independence was the first political shot fired at the status quo of governance. It was so radical in its philosophy that other nations, like France, used the fledgling nation as its role model. The result of this was the French Revolution, which followed in 1789, thirteen years later.

The Constitution of the United States of America was the second major document of the fledgling nation. Within it, the first 10 Amendments, known as the "Bill of Rights", became the second shot fired at "business as usual" governance methodologies around the world. Written by James Madison in response to a call by some states for a greater level of protection of individual rights and liberties, they provided specific limitations and prohibitions on governmental power. James Madison was greatly influenced by The Virginia Declaration of Rights, written by George Mason.

It is easy to recognize a pattern of response here. The original thirteen states were brought together in a reaction to the abuse of power foisted upon the colonists by King George III. The result of that was the Declaration of Independence. In order to protect the citizens of the United States against possible potential future abuses of power, even those, which could be committed against them by their own government, the Founding Fathers sought to anchor the rights of the individual in a form that guaranteed their protection. The result of this was the "Bill of Rights". The protection of the freedoms of the individual against the tyrannies of a rogue government was the main principal upon which the United States of America was founded and this principal was a direct reflection of the Protestant Christian basis of belief that the majority of those Founding Fathers espoused to. Citizen governance and the abolition of a "ruling class" made the United States unique among the nations of the world. It became such a feature of congress that an early list of senators and congressmen reads like a copy of "Who's Who" from the colonial times.

The sixteenth President of the United States, Abraham Lincoln, was a man devoted to the original principles of the United States of America. Elected into office during one of the most divisive periods of American History, his steadfast belief in the rights and liberties of the individual eventually led to the success of the Union Army over the Confederate Army in the Civil War. The end of that war brought with it the end of slavery. Freedom had been extended to the slaves. He was also a Christian who profoundly believed in a Creator. Personal tragedies and the hardships, which he faced throughout his life, ultimately led him down a path of deep and powerful faith. After the tragic death of his son Willie, who had declared that he wanted to become a preacher or teacher of the gospel, Abraham Lincoln developed a more intense and profound relationship with his Creator. A great testimony to this change occurred in the year 1863, the year immediately after the death of his son.

It was the year of the Thanksgiving Proclamation. Sarah Josepha Hale, the 74-year-old editor of Godey's Lady's Book, had called for a national day of Thanksgiving. After having unsuccessfully tried to convince many of President Lincoln's predecessors to create a permanent day of Thanksgiving in the national calendar, she made another attempt. Lincoln responded immediately and, after having commissioned William Seward, who was the Secretary of State, to write the proclamation, he signed it into law on October 3rd, 1863. The first part of the document begins with a listing of all of the successes of the previous year. It then continues:

> *"The country, rejoicing in the consciousness of augmented strength and vigor, is permitted to expect continuance of years with large increase of freedom.*
> *No human counsel hath devised nor hath any mortal hand worked out these great things. They are the gracious gifts of the Most High God, who, while dealing with us in anger for our sins, hath nevertheless remembered mercy.*
> *It has seemed to me fit and proper that they should be solemnly, reverently and gratefully acknowledged as with one heart and one voice by the whole American People.*
> *I do therefore invite my fellow citizens in every part of the United States, and also those who are at sea and those who are sojourning in foreign lands, to set apart and observe the last Thursday of November next, as a day of Thanksgiving and Praise to our beneficent Father*

who dwelleth in the Heavens. And I recommend to them that while offering up the ascriptions justly due to Him for such singular deliverances and blessings, they do also, with humble penitence for our national perverseness and disobedience, commend to His tender care all those who have become widows, orphans, mourners or sufferers in the lamentable civil strife in which we are unavoidably engaged, and fervently implore the interposition of the Almighty Hand to heal the wounds of the nation and to restore it as soon as may be consistent with the Divine purposes to the full enjoyment of peace, harmony, tranquility and Union." [16]

Where other Presidents had ignored the request, Abraham Lincoln picked up and formalized the tradition started by George Washington on the exact same day, 74 years earlier. The values, principles and traditions were passed from one generation to another in that act.

It was also the year of the Battle of Gettysburg, and the burial of all of the fallen soldiers on that field. The dedication of that field, where the soldiers were put to rest, brought forth a speech that has been called one of the greatest and most influential statements of national purpose ever written in the English language. Abraham Lincoln wrote the address himself, as he was traveling by train from Washington, D.C. to Gettysburg and the ceremony:

"Four score and seven years ago our fathers brought forth on this continent a new nation, conceived in liberty, and dedicated to the proposition that all men are created equal.
Now we are engaged in a great civil war, testing whether that nation, or any nation so conceived and so dedicated, can long endure. We are met on a great battlefield of that war…It is for us the living, rather, to be dedicated here to the unfinished work which they who fought here have thus far so nobly advanced. It is rather for us to be here dedicated to the great task remaining before us—that from these honored dead we take increased devotion to that cause for which they gave the last full measure of devotion—that we here highly resolve that these dead shall not have died in vain—that this nation, under God, shall have a new birth of freedom—and that government of the people, by the people, for the people, shall not perish from the earth." [17]

December of 1863 brought the inclusion of the motto "In God We Trust" on all coins minted in the United States. The idea stemmed from the Secretary of the Treasury, but offers yet another example of a consistent set of values being implemented by the government at all levels and in all aspects of life. It is clear, in this case, that the source of the values was not the Government Mountain. Instead, it was the continuation of values established by the Pilgrims and carried down through the generations.

The Business Mountain

Purpose:

- To seek out innovative and creative efforts in other mountains.
- To help creative efforts from other mountains reach markets.
- To serve the public and the Earth, by providing goods and services that cover a particular need or provide a tangible demonstration of the chosen values of society.
- To give direction, guidance and encourage market initiatives.
- To place the value and helpfulness of products and services above the profit motivation.

The primary purpose of the Business Mountain is to interact with other spheres of influence in order to seek out creative and innovative products and services. After having found these innovations, then the job of the Business Mountain is to assist those advancements in reaching the market they were created to serve. Business Mountain members coming alongside market initiatives and extending encouragement, direction, guidance and know-how can also accomplish this goal. It is essential for this mountain to place a higher value on the helpfulness and service to the public and to the Earth in general above the profit motivation. This must be done so that improvement in quality of life for people and the planet they live on can be assured.

Darkness

The period of Germany history in which Hitler was in power and the NSDAP ideology was the only possible option for governance offers the clearest negative example of how the Kingdom structure can be implemented to impact every sphere and every aspect of society. As with all of the other mountains, the Nazi party did not make an exception when it came to the Business Mountain. And, analog to the process of implementation in the other mountains, the changes began slowly and gathered steam until business owners had no other option left, than to submit to the domination. The advent of the removal of citizen's rights from the Jewish people, the NSDAP had created the possibility of closing down Jewish owned and operated businesses. The persecution continued with the seizing of funds, goods and other assets. Through these measures, their means of earning a living and supporting themselves was taken away.

Most people are aware of the atrocities committed against the Jewish people by the Nazi party. A number of those are even cognoscente of the impact that the ideology of the party had on Jewish communities and businesses. What the majority don't realize is that those same measures were applied to all businesses, but most especially to those that seemed to be a threat to the goals and ambitions of the party. Large internationally known businesses, like the company that produced Nike sports shoes, were bullied and forced into submission by the power politics of the party. Only those businesses, that were loyal to the party (at least on the surface), were allowed to continue to produce their products. The value of the product for society or for the planet as a whole was not taken into consideration. Instead, even valuable business organizations were forced to change their leadership or ultimately forced into bankruptcy if their management was seen as a threat to the NSDAP.

Hitler's plan was to create a massive army in the German people and to use that army to retake territory lost through the Versailles Treaty and war reparations. In order to achieve this goal, there needed to be a huge industrial and economic engine driving it. As the preparations for WWII continued, businesses were encouraged to change their products to more closely fit this goal. As the war unfolded, most businesses changed their focus from producing peacetime products, to producing products needed by the war effort. They were essentially forced to do this by the economics of the time, since the machinery of war was the only customer able to purchase their goods. The Government Mountain in Nazi Germany had encroached upon the Business Mountain to such an extent, that the original purpose of that sphere of influence was lost.

The advancement of the Allied Armies caused another stress on the Business Mountain in Germany. Those businesses, which had not been destroyed through the bombardment of the cities from the air, were in danger of losing them through the destruction caused by the ground forces. In the case of the company that later became Nike and Adidas, the arriving American army very nearly blew up their factory, when it was discovered that they had been producing weapons, instead of sports shoes. It was only the fact that one of the owners had specifically designed and produced the shoes that Jesse Owens wore during his legendary Olympic runs that saved that factory from destruction.

Light

Although generally taught otherwise, the colonists in Pre-Revolutionary America were not less well off than their counterparts in Europe. In fact, current research suggests that the average inhabitant of Colonial America was better off than his or her average English counterpart.[18] This fact gives cause to re-examine our understanding of the motivations leading up to the American Revolution, since poverty and lack was apparently not the mitigating factor.

The colonies were very lucrative. In the century between 1650 and 1750, scholars estimate that the gross national product (GNP) of British North America multiplied some 25 times.[19] It is even possible that people living in the American Colonies had the highest standard of living in the world at that time. This prosperity encouraged the Parliament in Britain to start devising unusual ways of tapping into and drawing from it. Some of the most creative taxation methods were the result. The Patriots responded by boycotting. Normally, economic prosperity is something that encourages passivity. People who are wealthy don't generally risk that to change a political system. Political instability costs money. This makes the situation in Colonial America all the more unusual. The proof of this can be found in the Declaration of Independence. The most prominent signature on that paper was John Hancock's and he was one of the wealthiest men in the thirteen colonies. So the economic prosperity in the colonies began long before the onset of the Revolutionary War. The foundational principles that governed the colonies and how they were managed, as well as the principles that governed everyday life set the stage for the production of wealth. Those principles stemmed from the Pilgrims who arrived on the Mayflower. They were carried down during that century through the families. They were also passed down through the education that the children received. And the tools of education used within the colonies included The New England Primer.

It is interesting to note that in Pre-Revolutionary America, the South, with its plantations and slaves, held and produced a greater portion of wealth than the North. The economy was predominantly agricultural in nature. Coastal towns and cities were primarily centers of trade. The richness of the land itself provided timber, rice and tobacco for export to the Caribbean and to Europe. The wealth of the colonists also increased demand for goods in the colonies themselves. The expansion into Western territories brought with it a wider range of available goods and that further increased both the demand and the overall level of prosperity of the colonists. The growing prosperity caused the British Government to look for innovative ways to tap into that wealth and re-distribute it to Britain. The tax on tea was met with boycotts and the Boston Tea Party. The tax on imported cloth led to the Homespun movement. During the Revolution the prosperity continued. Now, the farmers had the general population and not just one, but three armies to feed: the British army, the Patriot army, the French army, and their corresponding navies. Farmers and manufacturers of goods needed for the war were encouraged to take up debt through private lenders in a bid to increase production.

After the war, the newly formed United States of America experienced approximately two years of growth. Then, the government, the personal debt accumulation, and the destruction due to the war caught up with the economy and a severe depression was the result. This forced the newly created government into action and a National Bank was established to service the debt. Rioting, debt-ridden farmers were given relief through debt-forgiveness programs. The writing and adoption of the American Constitution in 1787 signaled the beginning of an economic turnaround and a period of tremendous and unprecedented growth and prosperity. The work laid a foundation for all future business dealings within the states. It formed a basis for the regulation of commerce and money through Congress; it opened the borders and created a free-trade zone. It also established the legal basis for protecting ideas and inventions. This allowed the open flow of goods and ideas between the states since there were no tariffs or taxes on interstate commerce and created an environment conducive to innovation.

These documents anchored the foundational values of freedom and individual liberties and opened the door to business in a scope and manner unknown until this point. The economic atmosphere yielded a 2% growth in productivity per year. The first cotton mill began production in 1790. The favorable patent regulations encouraged the invention of the cotton gin in 1793 and its patent in 1794, which paved the way for the expansion of the cotton industry and the growth of business in the nation.

The Arts and Entertainment Mountain

Purpose:

- To create places and situations in which people can relax, unwind and experience enjoyment.
- To be the prophetic mountain, allowing the future to be shown and discussed in the present.
- To be the sounding board for ideas from the other mountains.
- To provide a means for achieving insight and intellectual growth.
- To bring ideas and creativity to the public to facilitate social development, growth, and maturation.

The Arts and Entertainment Mountain is the most prophetic of the mountains. It is the launching stage for innovative and creative ideas that are then to be taken up and brought into reality through the other mountains. It is also the mountain in which enjoyable experiences and places for the recreation of people are fostered. A good example of this can be found in any one of a number of works of Science Fiction. These have existed throughout the ages, some of the most notable of which might be the works of H.G. Wells (1866-1946), the Hanna-Barbera cartoon, The Jetsons (1962-1963), and the original television show "Star Trek" which aired from 1966 until 1969 in the United States. In all of these works, products and innovations were introduced to the public through arts and entertainment and then became a reality many years later.

Although the list of these innovations is far too long to include in entirety, within this short discourse, here are a few examples taken from the various sources:

1. **The Communicator** – A hand-held device used to communicate between members of the Star Trek crew over great distances, or between the crew and their ship in orbit. It first appeared in the pilot episode in 1964. The hand-held mobile telephone, invented in 1973, is the modern equivalent to the Communicator.

2. **The Tanning Bed** – First appearing to the general public in an episode of the Jetsons, the idea of the tanning bed goes back as far as the early 1900's, when attempts were made to heal patients through the application of artificially produced sunlight. Home tanning devices were sold during the 1930's and 1940's. In 1979 a German scientist, Friedrich Wolff, resurrected the idea and began producing the first viable all-over tanning device, distributed worldwide.

3. **The Laser** – In H.G. Wells' *War of the Worlds* (1898), the invading aliens kill people with a heat ray described as "an almost noiseless and blinding flash of light". It is hard to find a more accurate layman's description of a laser, or "light amplification by stimulated emission of radiation", which was first invented by Theodore H. Maiman at the Hughes Research Laboratories located in Malibu, California, in 1960.

The highest form of arts and entertainment provides a means for achieving insight or intellectual growth. When the serious side of entertainment is explored, advancement and development result. Arts and entertainment provide a means for advancing creativity and innovation and bringing it to the public to facilitate societal development, growth and maturation. This is its purpose in the mountain hierarchy.

Darkness

Most people have no idea that Adolf Hitler was a frustrated artist. His greatest ambition in life was to become a professional. In 1907 and 1908, in an attempt to pursue that dream he took the entrance exams for admission to the prestigious Academy of Fine Arts in Vienna. He failed both of them. In his first exam, he passed the first portion of the exam and it was thought that he had a greater talent for architecture than for painting. In order to gain admission to the school of architecture, he would have had to complete secondary school, which he had quit a few years earlier. Because he had no intention of going back to complete his schooling, his dream of becoming a recognized artist died. Taking this piece of historical fact into consideration, many of Hitler's following actions take on another light.

In August of 1939, before the outbreak of WWII, Hitler is quoted as having told the British ambassador that he was an artist and saw himself as such. When the Polish question was settled, so the account of the ambassador, Hitler would retire as an artist.[20] Hitler saw himself as an architect as well as an artist. Because of this, he took an avid and personal interest in matters related to art and the art world during the time of the NSDAP. After Hitler's appointment as Chancellor on January 31st, 1933, he personally took immediate action to impact the art world and to "free" the German people of degeneracy that he felt had invaded that area of society. The result was book burnings, the dismissal of certain artists and musicians from prominent teaching positions, and the replacement of museum curators by loyal Party members.[21] By September of that same year, Hitler had created the "Reichskulturkammer" (Reich's Chamber of Culture) and had appointed Joseph Goebbels, who was also the Minister of Propaganda, as the administrator.

Five years after the party had gained total control of the political arena in Germany, the Nazi party organized two parallel art exhibitions. These took place from July to November 1937 and Hitler opened both of them. Both were designed to sway public opinion as to the value of certain types of artistic expression. On July 18th, 1937, Hitler gave a speech at the opening of the Great German Art Exhibition one day before the opening of the second exhibition, called the "Degenerate Art" exhibition. In it, he declared "merciless war" on cultural disintegration and attacked "chatterboxes, dilettantes and art swindlers".[22] The Nazi party confiscated 16,000 works of art during 1937 and 1938. These were taken from museums throughout Germany. The works of art then formed the basis for the "Degenerate Art" exhibition. They had been chosen on the basis of Hitler's evaluation of what was unacceptably "modern" and were defined as works that "insult German feeling, or destroy or confuse natural form or simply reveal an absence of adequate manual and artistic skill."[23]

The purpose of these art exhibitions was twofold. The first show, the Great German Art Exhibition, educated the public on what was acceptable art. Its counterpart, The Degenerate Art Exhibition, showed the visitors what was not acceptable art. Over one million people attended the exhibition in the first six weeks of showings and 650 works of art were displayed at that event. The Great German Art Exhibition in 1937 was the first of eight annual shows highlighting works approved by Hitler and the Nazi party. It set out to abolish any support and usage of Modernism, Expressionism, Dada, New Objectivity, Futurism and Cubism, streams of expression that had been developing since 1910.[24]

Hitler and the Nazi party were active in determining the officially accepted form of all types of art and expression. They worked in the realm of music; determining which artists were allowed to perform and which were not. Architecture also played a role in the officially sanctioned Nazi form of expression. Albert Speer, Hitler's architect once recounted, "Hitler quite often told me: 'You are fulfilling my dream. I would like to have been an architect. Fate made me the bildhauer Deutschlands, the sculptor of Germany. I would have liked to be Germany's architect. But I can't: you are. Even when I am dead you will go on, and I give you all my authority so that even after I am dead you will continue.' "[25] Hitler and the Nazi party recognized the impact of arts and entertainment on society and sought every means possible to use it to influence culture.

Light

There were two great movements in the realm of arts and entertainment that affected America during the period before and after the Revolution. The first was the age of Colonial Architecture and Art, which lasted until the Revolutionary War. The second was the time of Neoclassicism, which marked the beginning of the United States of America. The war was the delineation between the two. This transition was noticeable even on the level of the individual artist.

Where the Pre-Revolutionary period was marked by the arduous creation of individual and extremely creative works, the Post-Revolutionary era was highlighted by the influence of the coming Industrial Age. The artist was able to hire additional apprentices and the output of the shop increased considerably. The incorporation of machines to standardize production brought with it a new level of affluence, but it also reduced the amount of individual creativity displayed by the artists.

Paul Revere, the heroic silversmith of the Revolution was no exception in this transition.[26] His work also showed the clear distinction between the two epochs. His Pre-Revolutionary works were completed in the flamboyant Rococo style. His work after the Revolution was primarily Neo-Classical. With the help of a flatting mill, which helped to standardize the production of sheet silver, Paul Revere was able to increase the number of objects produced in his shop.

Presidents George Washington and Thomas Jefferson were instrumental in bringing about the adoption of Neoclassicism as the official artistic and architectural style in the fledgling republic. The mode had actually begun in Europe. Through publications brought from England praising its virtues it began to gain favor in the colonies. All of this corresponded with the time period of the Revolutionary War. And, when it was time to plan the Capitol of the new republic and its many official buildings, Neoclassicism was chosen because of its associations with the ancient civilizations of Rome and Greece. These societies were perceived as being strong and democratic and therefore worthy of emulation.

The growth in the popularity of Neoclassicism ran parallel to the rise of the Age of Enlightenment. The Reformation of the Catholic Church, which began when Martin Luther nailed the 95 Theses on the door of the Wittenberg Palace Church in 1517, started the age. It spread via Gutenberg's printing press (1439). The printing press revolutionized the process of passing knowledge and information from one place to the other and was instrumental in empowering the change in thought fueled by radical ideas of freedom from tyranny and the protection of individual rights.

The push of the 16th century towards individual rights and the overthrow of tyrannical institutions led to the beginning of rationalism, as espoused by René Descartes (1596-1650). In his theology, Descartes insisted upon the absolute freedom of God's act of creation. Descartes then passed the baton to John Locke (1632-1704), son of devout Puritans, who wrote many works of political as well as philosophical importance. This culminated in perhaps his most well-known work of political philosophy published in 1689, titled *"Two Treatises of Government: In the Former, The False Principles, and Foundation of Sir Robert Filmer, and His Followers, Are Detected and Overthrown. The Latter Is an Essay Concerning The True Original, Extent, and End of Civil Government,"* or, more simply just **Two Treatises of Government.** The first treatise attacked patriarchalism.

The second included an outline of Locke's vision for a more civilized society based upon the natural rights of the individual and the theory of Social Contract, which argues that the individual has consented, in some fashion or other to surrender some of their individual freedoms to the authority of a ruler or the decision of the majority in exchange for the protection of their remaining rights and liberties.[27] The French form of the treatise came into the hands of French philosophers Montesquieu (1689-1755), Voltaire (1694-1778), and Jean-Jacques Rousseau (1712-1778). Searching historic documents of the colonial pre-American Revolutionary period, scholars determined that the Founding Fathers quoted Montesquieu more frequently with respect to government and politics than any other source except the Bible. The Bible was still the primary source.[28] Montesquieu, who attended the Catholic College of Juilly from 1700 to 1711, believed in a government that distributed the power to govern among different entities and that a clearly defined and balanced separation of powers was imperative, when attempting to create a stable government. After being confronted with the political philosophical treatise of John Locke, Rousseau then published his own book almost a hundred years after it was originally published, in 1762, entitled **The Social Contract** (Du contrat social ou Principes du droit politique). It also covered the idea of an implied political contract between the governing and the governed.

The evolution of political philosophical thought from the Protestant Reformation until the founding of the United States of America was a slow, but steady development in the art of political philosophy, since philosophy is an art and not a science.[29] The etymological meaning of the word "philosophy" is "the love of wisdom". This advancement, therefore, could easily be classified as an incremental growth in the wisdom of good governance. The result of the application of that wisdom was a new form of governance, never having been tried on the Earth before. It brought with it a whole new way of thinking, a new set of values and these thoughts then began to manifest as a reality in all spheres of society. From the churches, to the schools, to the businesses, to the artists' workshops, this new value system and thought system touched every aspect of life.

Ultimately, it was reflected onto the solid physical form of the built environment as Neoclassicism. Neoclassicism was a reflection of the political phenomenon of Enlightenment and Enlightenment built upon the ideals of republicanism and self-government found in Ancient Greece and Rome. It made sense that the built environment of a new republic and all of the official buildings of the Capitol would reflect that heritage of thought, through external expression. Neoclassical architecture combines elements of both Federal architecture, which is based upon Roman architecture of ancient times and Greek revival architecture, which includes elements of classic Greek architecture. It was the single most important architectural style of the late 18th and early 19th centuries. The United States Capitol Building, which began construction in 1793, is perhaps the single greatest example of this style of architecture. Thomas Jefferson was the main proponent of the use of this architectural style for the Capitol and he made certain it would have all of the grandeur befitting a Roman "spherical" temple created to house the Congress of the new republic.

The Greco-Roman architectural style of the buildings was superimposed on an expansive, unilateral Baroque plan for the city, created in 1791 by the French artist and engineer, Major Pierre Charles L'Enfant.[30] This was a hitherto unheard of situation. The United States created a capital for its newly born republic on land that had never been built upon and was bare. It is the only nation to have had the opportunity to create its nation's capital in this manner. It is a singularly unique national capital built for a nation founded upon political philosophical principals birthed in the Protestant Reformation and matured through centuries of "the love of" wisdom and the search for the same.

The Media Mountain

Purpose:

- To provide a platform to showcase unusual and creative solutions and events in all of the other mountains.
- To be a source of technologies, that help to connect diverse people from various geographical locations.
- To build up, support and move creative solutions and events in the other mountains forward.
- To be a vehicle for the other mountains to use to educate.
- To spread knowledge about the divine purpose and structure of society.

The Media Mountain is the last of the mountains in the Kingdom. In the Bible it states that the last will be first and the first will be last. It also states that the greatest will be the servant to all (Matthew 20:26, 23:11; Luke 22:26).

The Media Mountain was created to serve all of the other mountains. Its job is to come alongside the other mountains and to highlight innovations in those spheres of influence by supporting their activities through the spread of information. The Media Mountain supports innovations, by educating and informing about those innovations. It is called to serve the other spheres of influence, by informing about initiatives in those spheres and connecting individual initiatives together. It is called to serve the others by being vigilant in developing technologies that support and improve communication means and methods. Through that service to the others, it has the capacity to be the greatest of the mountains.

Darkness

The Reichsministerium für Volksaufklärung und Propaganda or Reich Ministry of Public Enlightenment and Propaganda was established on March 14th, 1933 just nine days after the NSDAP received 43,9% of the vote in the general elections. The first order of business after the election was to place a ban on the Communist party the day after the elections. The second order of business was to establish a ministry for propaganda and 10 days after that; Hitler was declared dictator for four years on the 24th of March.

The creation of a ministry to spread propaganda was only one step in an intricate plan devised by Hitler and the NSDAP to infiltrate every social arena. The strategy was to elevate the Nazi ideology to a premier position as the only acceptable source of values for the nation. All other schools of thought were either banned, or systematically rotted out.

Hitler put Reich Minister Joseph Goebbels in charge of the ministry. The ministry was created to "centralize Nazi control of all aspects of German cultural and intellectual life".[31] Organized into seven directorates, the Reich Ministry of Public Enlightenment and Propaganda served to regulate the culture and mass media of a NSDAP controlled Germany. It supervised broadcasting in all forms, including the NEWS distribution networks. Together with the Chamber of Culture (Reichskulturkammer) and the institution devoted to cinematography, the Chamber of Film (Reichsfilmkammer) it managed and regulated filmmaking, theater events, music, visual arts, literature, and all other avenues of media and broadcasting. No thought, no piece of literature, no artwork, no piece of literature or theatrical work was allowed to be presented or released to the public, if it wasn't approved by the ministry in advance.

During the Nazi period, the media was not an independent entity designed to broadcast current events in an unbiased manner. Instead, it served as a vehicle to further the ideology of the NSDAP. Hitler laid out the system for achieving his media/propaganda objective in two segments of his book, Mein Kampf. Hitler writes:

"Propaganda must always address itself to the broad masses of the people. (...) All propaganda must be presented in a popular form and must fix its intellectual level so as not to be above the heads of the least intellectual of those to whom it is directed. (...) The art of propaganda consists precisely in being able to awaken the imagination of the public through an appeal to their feelings, in finding the appropriate psychological form that will arrest the attention and appeal to the hearts of the national masses. The broad masses of the people are not made up of diplomats or professors of public jurisprudence nor simply of persons who are able to form reasoned judgment in given cases, but a vacillating crowd of human children who are constantly wavering between one idea and another. (...) The great majority of a nation is so feminine in its character and outlook

*that its thought and conduct are ruled by sentiment rather than by
sober reasoning. This sentiment, however, is not complex, but simple
and consistent. It is not highly differentiated, but has only the negative
and positive notions of love and hatred, right and wrong, truth and
falsehood."*[32]

In the second segment of his book, Hitler explains the way in which
propaganda can be unilaterally disseminated:

*"Propaganda must not investigate the truth objectively and, in so far
as it is favorable to the other side, present it according to the
theoretical rules of justice; yet it must present only that aspect of the
truth which is favorable to its own side. (...) The receptive powers of
the masses are very restricted, and their understanding is feeble. On
the other hand, they quickly forget. Such being the case, all-effective
propaganda must be confined to a few bare essentials and those must
be expressed as far as possible in stereotyped formulas. These slogans
should be persistently repeated until the very last individual has come
to grasp the idea that has been put forward. (...) Every change that is
made in the subject of a propagandist message must always emphasize
the same conclusion. The leading slogan must of course be illustrated
in many ways and from several angles, but in the end one must always
return to the assertion of the same formula."*[33]

At this point I would like to thank the anonymous Wikipedia editor who
compressed the text of Mein Kampf into the two quotes that I have included.

After the creation of the propaganda ministry, Hitler and Goebbels
systematically removed dissenting voices from the public eye and from the
press. They then replaced those voices with ones that were more in keeping
with the ideology of the NSDAP. This happened in all forms of media: print,
radio broadcasts, and film.

Their strongest weapon, however, was the radio. Programs were broadcast
both internally and externally and had a carefully crafted content. The
internal broadcasts offered a steady diet of war news, anti-Jewish rhetoric,
and programs designed to educate the citizens of Germany to expectations
placed upon them by the NSDAP. German citizens were, in part, being
trained to be "good Nazis" through the radio broadcast programming. The

external propaganda broadcasts, known throughout the world as "Germany Calling", targeted audiences in the United Kingdom and the United States. The programs were translated into approximately 30 different languages and sent via shortwave. Initially, the broadcasts served to present the NSDAP slant on the NEWS to foreign nationals. Later, they openly attacked the influence of Jews on the politics of the US and of Great Britain as well as the leaders of both nations. To attract and keep an international audience, it offered the opportunity for prisoners of war to send greetings to friends and family members on air. Understandably, this made the program particularly popular with listeners in the allied nations, most especially the US and the UK. After the war, the broadcasters were rounded up and either executed or sentenced to jail for their participation in the radio broadcasts. The criminal offence was treason. "Germany Calling" was shut down when the British Army reached Hamburg on April 30th, 1945.

Light

The right to a free and independent press in the Colonies of America was hard-won. British magistrates and appointed authorities viewed a free-press as a nuisance and hindrance of the aims of the government. The Virginia Governor, William Berkeley, wrote of the idea of free press in 1671,

> *"I thank God, there are no free schools nor printing and I hope we shall not have, these hundred years, for learning has brought disobedience, and heresy, and sects into the world, and printing has divulged them, and libels against the best government. God keep us from both."* [34]

The British government recognized the power of a free press and did everything it could to hinder the transportation of information and ideas at a large scale. By the late 1600's, it realized that it would not be able to hinder written NEWS and issued the first license to a printer. Licenses insured that the government had a hand in who was allowed to print things and, just as easily as it was issued, a license could also be revoked. Printing papers became very lucrative and the threat of removal of license was enough to restrain most of the "enthusiasm" of the printers.

Setting an example was also a successful way of curtailing the freedom of the press. The first license to publish a newspaper was issued in 1690 to

Benjamin Harris. Publishing his debut newspaper, Harris reported that the English military forces had allied themselves with the "miserable" savages. Four days later the affronted British authorities revoked his license and **Boston's Publick Occurrences Both Forreign and Domestick** went out of business. It was the first newspaper of the colonies and lasted a total of 5 days.

A history of the whole of the newspaper business during the pre and post-Revolutionary War period in America can be seen through a study of the history of the Franklin family. In 1717, James Franklin, older brother of Benjamin Franklin returned from a voyage to England carrying a printing press and letters. His intent was to set up a business as a printer in Boston. Upon receiving his license, James founded the **New-England Courant**. At the insistence of his father, Benjamin then indentured himself to his brother at the age of twelve.

This instilled in him a love of the craft. Unfortunately, in a situation similar to that of Benjamin Harris, James Franklin also lost his license and spent a month in jail after one of the articles that he printed offended the Assembly. In order to avoid having the newspaper shut down, Benjamin Franklin's name was put on it and James' name was taken off. James continued to work for the paper, although Ben was the official publisher and proprietor of the newspaper.

Eventually, Benjamin Franklin returned to Philadelphia in 1726 and opened his first print shop. The shop produced a range of materials, among which were currency, books, government pamphlets and leaflets. This was the start of a chain of print shops and post offices, which spread up and down the East Coast of America. In 1729, he purchased the **Pennsylvania Gazette** with a business partner. Later, he founded **Poor Richard's Almanac**, which was an annual publication of common sense and useful wisdom. Both publications offered ample opportunity for Franklin to report on events and educate the masses. He also wrote for both publications, often using a pseudonym.

His influence on the sentiments in the colonies can clearly be demonstrated through his Gazette publications of 1739-1741. It was the period of the First Great Awakening in the colonies and the arrival of a young Anglican preacher, George Whitefield, offered plenty of material to fill Franklin's publications and to encourage the sales of advertising in those papers. Hugely popular, he drew crowds wherever he preached. Although Benjamin Franklin was raised in the home of pious Puritans, he was a Deist and rarely attended church. Franklin became such an arduous supporter of Whitefield, that he printed all of his sermons on the front page of the *Gazette*. In fact, Franklin devoted 45 issues to Whitefield's activities, while he was in the colonies. He also used his influence as a publisher to print all of the preacher's journals. Franklin remained a supporter and the two men remained friends until Whitefield died in 1770.

Benjamin Franklin was also a major figure within the postal system. Initially, the British appointed him as postmaster of Philadelphia in 1737. By 1753, he had become the joint postmaster general for all of the American colonies. His position as postmaster gave him access to all news materials coming into and going out of the colonies, the primary source of information of the day. This established and strengthened his position as the foremost agent for up-to-date information and provided his newspapers with plenty of material to publish. While postmaster, he also implemented different measures to improve the functionality of the postal system. Franklin held the position of postmaster general until 1774, when the British determined that he was too sympathetic to the Patriot cause and colonial interests. The Continental Congress, taking over the governmental functions from the British, appointed Franklin as the first postmaster general of the United States of America in July of 1775. This position gave him authority over all post offices from Massachusetts to Georgia. He held the position until November of 1776.

Carol Humphrey, Professor of Journalism at the Oklahoma Baptist University and Secretary of the American Journalism Historian's Association, stated, "Newspapers existed primarily to inform people of what was going on in the rest of the world, prior to the Revolution."[35] The advent of the Revolution changed that focus. Now, political events within the colonies themselves became the focus and many of the publications began to report on events in such a manner, as to support the cause of the Patriots.

During the French and Indian War, Benjamin Franklin created the first cartoon to be carried in an American newspaper. The picture featured a snake cut into eight sections. Each section of the snake represented one of the colonies or a region of the colonies and the caption under the picture read: "Join, or Die". It was published on May 9th, 1754. Franklin published the cartoon along with an editorial complaining about the "disunited state" of the colonies. Although the image emerged during the French and Indian War as an appeal for unity with Great Britain to defeat the enemy, by 1765 it became a symbol for colonial unity and freedom during the Revolutionary War, when the caption under the image was changed to "Unite or Die".

The Stamp Act was a further impetus for the redirection of reporting in Colonial newspapers. The account of the Boston Massacre, carried by the Boston Gazette in 1770, signaled the end of British influence on the content of printed materials. As feared by the British, the prosperity and the expanse of Benjamin Franklin's news empire became an enemy and a "great inconvenience" to the British cause. The success of the Patriots during the Revolutionary war was due, in great part, to the increasing freedom afforded the press in the colonies. Daily newspaper publications began in the 1780's and by 1790, there were about a hundred papers being printed in the colonies. It was a period of great press freedom and this freedom was often used on behalf of one political party or the other. Both the Federalist and the Republican parties subsidized their own press publications.

In addition to reporting on the news of the conflict, papers also began to print lengthy editorials arguing for or against political positions. Pamphlets and broadsides were produced to rally sentiments for the cause of the Patriots. Many of these written works were instrumental in altering the opinion of those that had remained neutral. Some of the most influential of these voices were women. The First Lady of Pennsylvania, Esther De Berdt Reed, was one of these voices. Reaching for her pen in 1780, she wrote and published a broadside calling for all Patriot women to rise up and support General Washington and his army when their situation was so dire and they were in short of supplies. Her publication "The Sentiments of an American Woman" was able to animate the colonists so much, that she raised a whopping $ 300,000 for the Continental Army.

Other voices, like Mercy Otis Warren, who was known as the "Conscience of the American Revolution", expressed opinions by writing them down. She was an extremely prolific writer and her works influenced many people. Her ideas, thoughts, and opinions on wars and other political issues were put on paper over the span of a lifetime and she also achieved the honor of being the first woman playwright in America. Her sympathy for the American Revolution and her views on it propelled her to compose extensive amounts of political poetry.[36] The growth in freedom in press and publications, which resulted from the loss of control of the news through the British, allowed works like those of Mercy Otis Warren and many others to be printed and widely distributed throughout the colonies.

There were newspapers that served every conceivable political party and ideology in the 1790's. The editors of those newspapers were convinced that they were serving their readers by supporting their particular party through everything that they incorporated in their newspapers. This included writing editorials and essays that reflected the party ideology. It also consisted of writing scathing articles that attacked the opposition. Two examples of this were the *National Gazette*, which was written and published for the Jeffersonian Republicans; and the *Gazette of the United States*, which was written and published for the Hamiltonian Federalists. Along with the publishers and editors that kept watch over the integrity of the message, government officials and political figures often took to writing for the papers, in order to present their way of thinking on policies. They did this anonymously and adopted pseudonyms so that they could write without public criticism of their person. Benjamin Franklin, Alexander Hamilton, James Madison, and many others, often expressed themselves in this manner.

Samuel Adams said of free press in 1768, "there is nothing so fretting and vexatious, nothing so justly terrible to tyrants…as a free press." Slightly less than 20 years later, Thomas Jefferson added, "were it left to me to decide whether we should have a government without newspapers or newspapers without a government, I should not hesitate a moment to prefer the latter." The necessity of a free press was so ingrained into the American psyche, that John Adams included a guarantee of liberty of the press when he wrote "A Constitution or Form of Government for the Commonwealth of Massachusetts" in 1779.

In an effort to quickly establish a legal basis for the newly formed United States of America, the US Constitution was hurriedly written and ratified by

September 17th, 1787. The document immediately added to that Constitution was the Bill of Rights (the first 10 Amendments to the Constitution), which came into effect four years and three months later on December 15th, 1791. The first of the ten rights or liberties to be included in that document was:

> ***Congress shall make no law respecting an establishment of religion, or prohibiting the free exercise thereof; or abridging the freedom of speech, or of the press; or the right of the people peaceably to assemble, and to petition the Government for a redress of grievances.***
> — *The First Amendment to the U.S. Constitution*

Through this Amendment to the Constitution of the United States of America, the Founding Fathers guaranteed and protected the most cherished and prized liberties of men.

Author's note: Throughout history, the right to a free and open press and the right to the open expression of thought are the first rights to be suppressed within any society moving towards an authoritarian form of government. Thought leaders and dissenting voices are rounded up and silenced. Books with alternative viewpoints are banned, gathered, and burned. The truth, sought by investigative journalists, and spread through underground newspapers, is systematically quashed. The path towards a dictatorial society has historically been built upon the suppression of free speech. The world is currently going through a period of unprecedented shifting and shaking. A sober look at current events reveals a disturbing trend towards repeating these past historic patterns.

Summary

This chapter was included in the book so that readers will understand how God's Kingdom is designed to function on Earth. The first part of the chapter presented the five ranks in God's Kingdom army, explained the functions that each rank has, and then talked about how each of the ranks works together to further the Kingdom. The second part examined and explained the eight spheres of influence, by taking two examples from history and using them as case studies. By doing this, you, the reader, were taken on a journey through all of the mountains and given a clear illustration of how God's Kingdom can work. One of the cases was the example of Nazi

Germany, which highlighted the damage that can result when the Kingdom structure is used for evil purposes. The other model was the example of the founding of the United States of America.

The cases were presented so that a reader could go through each mountain or sphere of influence and clearly recognize the effects of using God's design for good, or misusing it. I really can't take credit for coming up with this methodology for presenting the Kingdom structure to you. The inspiration for this came out of a particularly concentrated period of prayer. Jesus often used parables when explaining Kingdom concepts. His parables usually began with statements like, "The Kingdom of Heaven is like…".

I also believe that The Lord was making the process interesting for me, by using historical events. Both examples serve to make the Kingdom system clear and recognizable to almost everyone. Using Nazi Germany makes the consequences for the misuse of the Kingdom system apparent and the use of the founding of the USA makes the benefits of using the Kingdom structure for good obvious.

The Kingdom structural system is a law. It functions equally for the forces of darkness and the light. And scripture backs this up. "In that way, you will be acting as true children of your Father in heaven. For He gives His sunlight to both the evil and the good, and He sends rain on the just and the unjust alike" (Matthew 5:45, NLV). Jesus explained it further in Mark 4:26-29, when He said that the Kingdom of God is like seed scattered on the ground by man. Whether that man is good or evil, whether the intentions of that person or government are good or evil, it is irrelevant. That seed will grow day and night and eventually, it will yield a harvest.

Germany, during the NSDAP era, offers a shocking example of the use of the Kingdom structure to support a dark system. It is only one of many more examples. Stalin utilized the same methodology to promote his ideology. In fact, nearly every dictator has utilized this procedure to supplant an existing national culture and national values with his own.

Today, we are faced with the growing understanding that in many nations of the world the hijacked Kingdom system is being used to usurp Christian values, norms and cultures. In an attempt to replace them with other ideologies ranging from Islam to secular Humanism, governments and non-governmental organizations are systematically attacking Christians and Christian organizations, restricting practice and expression of faith. In the worst cases, as was clearly shown within the ISIS caliphate, Christians were systematically being hunted down and murdered.[37] In Nigeria, Boko Haram is hunting down and invading Christian villages, where they routinely slaughter whole villages.[38]

In addition to the violent oppression of the Christian faith in many nations, other supposedly more advanced nations use their legal systems to restrict and shut down the free exercise of Christian beliefs and expression of values. The Covid 19 pandemic crisis of 2020 served to expose many of these practices by forcing them out in the open. In many states throughout the United States churches were shut down, while pot dispensaries, liquor stores, and mass riotous gatherings were allowed. Public gatherings were restricted in size but special restrictions were placed on church meetings. In California a universal ban on church services was put in place that went so far as to restrict Bible studies in homes.[39] It was a clear expression of values. Individual, God-given, and Constitutionally protected rights were suppressed and restricted by political individuals using the crisis to force their personal ideologies on others. If you want to find out where you fit in the Kingdom structure go here:

https://identitypassport.thrivecart.com/kingdom-come-passport/

---

[1] *"The Mayflower Compact (1620)" (PDF). www.cos.edu.*

[2] http://www.law.ou.edu/hist/orders.html

[3] http://www.adherents.com/gov/Founding_Fathers_Religion.html

[4] https://en.wikipedia.org/wiki/The_1619_Project

[5] https://nypost.com/2020/01/24/scholars-are-eviscerating-the-new-york-times-1619-project/

[6] Gadsden, Christopher, "To the Planters, Mechanics, and Freeholders of the Province of South Carolina, No Ways Concerned in the Importation of British Manufactures", June 22, 1789.

[7] Faragher, John Mack, et al. Out of Many: A History of the American People. Upper Saddle River, New Jersey: Pearson Prentice Hall, 2006.

[8] http://www.edenton.com/history/miscfact.htm

[9] *Jacqueline Beatty. "Ladies Association of Philadelphia". Retrieved 2016-05-09.*

[10] *Berkin, Carol (1997). First Generations: Women In Colonial American. New York: Hill and Wang.*

[11] http://www.britannica.com/topic/The-New-England-Primer

[12] http://www.bartleby.com/101/435.html

[13] The New England Primer, 1750 ed., p. 28

[14] http://www.archives.gov/exhibits/charters/declaration_transcript.html

[15] McPherson, James. *Abraham Lincoln and the Second American Revolution.* New York: Oxford University Press, 1991. ISBN 0-19-505542-X, p. 126.

[16] http://www.abrahamlincolnonline.org/lincoln/speeches/thanks.htm

[17] Boritt, Gabor (2006). *The Gettysburg Gospel: The Lincoln Speech That Nobody Knows* Simon & Schuster. 432 pp. ISBN 0-7432-8820-3.

[18] http://voxeu.org/article/america-s-revolution-economic-disaster-development-and-equality

[19] Shmoop Editorial Team, "Economy in The American Revolution,"

Shmoop University, Inc., Last modified November 11, 2008, http://www.shmoop.com/american-revolution/economy.html.

[20] https://docs.google.com/forms/d/1Lzapxj-k6e7xnSg9yQLAlYJ13wyb7hAppmA0OT8OBzM/viewform?c=0&w=1&usp=mail_form_link

[21] Adam, Peter (1992). *Art of the Third Reich.* New York: Harry N. Abrams, Inc. ISBN 0-8109-1912-5, pg. 52.

[22] *Spotts, Frederic (2002). Hitler and the Power of Aesthetics. The Overlook Press. pp. 151–68. ISBN 1-58567-507-5.*

[23] Ibid.

[24] Barron, Stephanie, *Degenerate art: The Fate of the Avant-Garde in Nazi Germany* (Los Angeles, Calif.: Los Angeles County Museum of Art, 1991), 18.

[25] Hughes, Robert, "Of Gods and Monsters", The Guardian – Online, Friday, 31 January, 2003.

[26] Wees, Beth Carver. "Paul Revere, Jr. (1734–1818)." In *Heilbrunn Timeline of Art History.* New York: The Metropolitan Museum of Art, 2000–. http://www.metmuseum.org/toah/hd/rvre/hd_rvre.htm (October 2003)

[27] https://en.wikipedia.org/wiki/Two_Treatises_of_Government

[28] *Lutz, Donald S. (1984). "The Relative Influence of European Writers on Late Eighteenth-Century American Political Thought". American Political Science Review 78 (1): 189–197. doi:10.2307/1961257*

[29] Friedland, Julian, "Philosophy is Not a Science", The New York Times-The Stone, April 5, 2012, 8:30pm

[30] https://www.nps.gov/nr/travel/wash/lenfant.htm

[31] *Longerich, Peter (2015). Goebbels: A Biography. New York: Random House. ISBN 978-1400067510, pp. 212-213.*

^{32} Hitler, Adolf, Mein Kampf, translated into English by James Murphy, Project Gutenberg Australia, September 2002, Gutenberg.net.au/ebooks02/0200601.txt

^{33} Ibid.

^{34} Breig, James, Early American Newspapering, CW Journal, Spring 03. https://www.history.org/Foundation/journal/spring03/journalism.cfm

^{35} Breig, James, Early American Newspapering, CW Journal, Spring 03. https://www.history.org/Foundation/journal/spring03/journalism.cfm

^{36} Pamela Kline and Paul Pavao, "*Mercy Otis Warren,*" 2010-1013, accessed October 7, 2013, http://www.revolutionary-war.net/mercy-otis-warren.html.

^{37} https://www.pewresearch.org/fact-tank/2018/06/21/key-findings-on-the-global-rise-in-religious-restrictions/

^{38} https://www.genocidewatch.com/post/2020/04/13/nigeria-is-a-killing-field-of-defenseless-christians

^{39} https://www.washingtontimes.com/news/2020/jul/20/gavin-newsom-sued-over-ban-against-home-bible-stud/

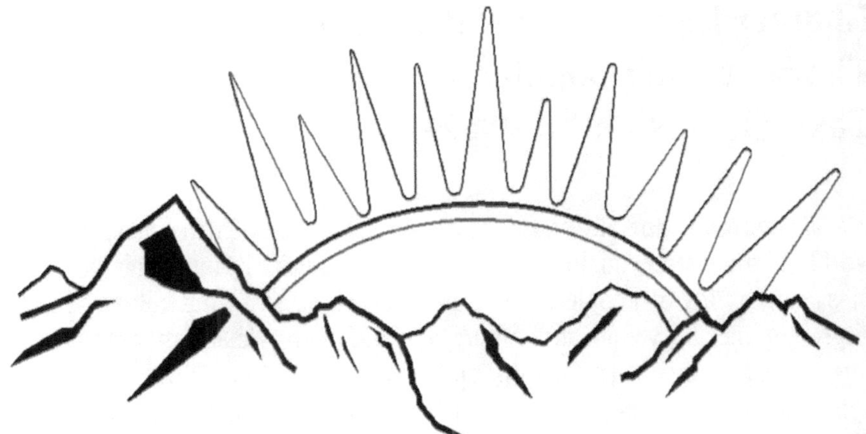

Chapter Eight – A New Beginning –
The Sons and Daughters
Take Their Rightful Places

We are currently in one of the most pivotal periods in the history of the world. Everywhere you look it seems like darkness is invading the Earth. Mass migrations of people are causing clashes between the values of those migrating and the values and culture of the countries that they are entering. International human trafficking and child abductions have reached an epidemic scale. Politics and clashes between parties have become brutally divisive. Whole nations are seeking to leave associations once thought to be insoluble. Even sections of countries or regions of countries are seeking to secede from parent countries. Governments are increasingly unstable and political unrest is growing.

Earthquakes, fires, and heat waves of immense proportions are affecting nations. Hail is falling in record-breaking sizes and volumes previously unheard of. Monumentally sized sinkholes are opening up in the Earth. Unusual sounds are being emitted from the earth and sky that defy scientific explanation. Rivers and waterways are turning red like blood, for no apparent reason. Flocks of birds are falling from the sky, dead and groups of marine mammals are washing up to shores around the world. In virtually every region of the Earth and in virtually every aspect of society, indications are that something is terribly amiss in our world. No typical politician seems to have the answer. In general, there is a universal lack of leadership in all areas of life. What we are witnessing is a monumental call to arms. For those of you unfamiliar with this term, the Merriam-Webster Dictionary defines "a call to arms" as:

1. A summons to engage in active hostilities
2. A summons, invitation, or appeal to undertake a particular course of action (a political call to arms).[1]

We are hearing, and seeing, a call to arms to the Body of Christ to rise up and take back territory relinquished to the enemy through years of neglect and passivity.

The whole Earth is groaning, waiting for the sons and daughters of God to step into their leadership position over the events, activities and systems of this planet (Romans 8:21-22). Adam was created and called to husband the Earth. He lost his position of authority over the Earth, when he sinned. Jesus, through His sacrifice on the Cross, became the perfect sacrifice and through that gift, retrieved that position of dominion and authority over the Earth from the enemy. It was then passed on to the sons and daughters of God. Unfortunately, the sons and daughters have been woefully unaware of their position and of their responsibility in God's plan to bring redemption to every living thing on the planet.

The plan of redemption was always designed as a plan of cooperation between God and man. He did His part and He is still waiting for us to do ours. For generations, the church has been taught that Jesus would sovereignly return to set up His Kingdom on Earth without our ever having to do anything, other than praying, to help. The reality is that Jesus has been waiting for the Body of Christ to step into its God given authority and "occupy until He returns"(Luke 19:13).

Ekklesia - The Church Moves out into The World

In Daniel 22:45, when Daniel explained the concept of a rock which grew to become a mountain and overtook the hills of the world, he was describing the faithful followers and doers of the words of Jesus. The mountain that he was describing was the mountain of the Kingdom of God on Earth (Micah 4:1, Isaiah 2:2). The prophecy states that all the Earth will stream to that mountain to look for advice and to follow the Lord's way of doing things. Specifically it states, "that He may teach us about His ways and that we may walk in His paths". This was to occur "in the last days". Not, as we have been taught, after the Body of Christ is raptured and Jesus returns.

This begs the question, who are the people that will be drawn to this mountain? The scripture says "nations" and "peoples". This is plural but not inclusive, because the scripture places a condition on the participation by saying "many nations" and not **all**. Participation in the process of bringing His Kingdom to Earth is voluntary. People must "choose" to participate; they will not be "forced" to participate. So, there will be a group of people or nations that choose to place God's way of doing things above man's way of doing things in the last days before Jesus returns. These people and nations will seek the wisdom of God to apply in their every day lives and as a method of ruling over every aspect of society. Another name for that group of people is the Body of Christ or ekklesia. Ekklesia is the rock that will grow to become a mountain and overtake the hills of the world.

The Greek word ekklesia (ἐκκλησίαν), is derived from the Greek terms "ek" which means "out from among", suggesting movement from the interior outwards and "kaleó", meaning "I call, summon or invite". Biblically, the Church, or ekklesia, is a group of people called (by God – **I call**) to come out from its grouping and to go out into society. Combined with the rock references within the same text, it denotes a grouping of people who base their lives and their actions upon the teachings of Jesus and the Holy Scripture called out from their place of gathering and called to move into the world affecting it with the principles and values upon which they have based their lives and their actions. The manifest sons and daughters of God, the ones that have chosen to follow the promptings and leadings of the Holy Spirit, will be the ones who establish God's way of doing things on Earth. They will be the ones to step out into every arena of life and positively impact those spheres of influence. They will be the leaders in life and the world will stream to them to understand how to implement Biblical values and God's way of doing things into every aspect of life. The Ekklesia will be the ones who usher in the age of the Basileia.

The relationship between the ekklesia (Church) and the basileia (Kingdom of God on Earth) is described in Matthew 16:19. In his book, *The Story that Chooses Us*, George Hunsberger examines this relationship: "One of the two points where Matthew's Gospel mentions "church" (ekklesia) underscores this distinction and begins to establish the interrelationship between the reign of God and the church: *"on this rock I will build my church,"* and then *"And I will give you the keys of the Kingdom"* (Matt. 16:16-19) Here it is clear that the church (ekklesia) and the reign of God (basileia) are separate conceptions, but also that the two are intimately bound together." Loc 1362 of 3807, Kindle Version.

Basileia – The Benevolent Kingdom on Earth

When Jesus taught His disciples to pray in Matthew 6:10, He admonished them to pray to God that *"your Kingdom come…on Earth as it is in Heaven"*. Jesus also taught them, in that verse, **how** God's Kingdom was to manifest on Earth: *"your Will be done on Earth as it is in Heaven"*.

Many in the Body of Christ believe that God's Kingdom will manifest as a result of a Rapture (Harpazo) and sovereign establishment of Jesus' reign through His return. As convenient as this viewpoint is, it is difficult to find the scriptural basis for this conviction. Instead, there are endless scriptural texts and Biblical accounts that establish the reality of a partnership between mankind and God: Genesis 1:26, Genesis 1:28, Genesis 18:16-33, Exodus 32:12-14, Judges 7, Matthew 25:21, Galatians 3:29, Galatians 4:7, Ephesians 3:6, Colossians 1:24, 2 Timothy 2:12, 1 Peter 4:13, Revelation 21:7.

The Kingdom (basileia) will come on Earth, when the church (ekklesia) begins to corporately submit to the Will of God in every aspect of their lives. "The church is constituted by those who are entering and receiving the reign of God. It is where the children of the reign corporately manifest the presence and characteristic features of God's reign. The divine reign expresses itself in a unique, though not exhaustive or exclusive, fashion in the church." Hunsberger, George R., The Story that Chooses Us, Loc 1399 of 3807, Kindle version.

The scripture is clear, that *"those who are led by the Spirit of God are the children of God"* (Romans 8:14). The children of God are the members of the ekklesia who have submitted themselves to the leadings of the Holy Spirit (Romans 8:16). This is a clear prerequisite to being able to be used by The Spirit to manifest the Kingdom of God on Earth, as it is not possible for a person with divided loyalties to step into that authority. *"What agreement is there between the temple of God and idols? For we are the temple of the living God. As God has said: 'I will live with them and walk among them, and I will be their God, and they will be my people.'"* 2 Corinthians 6:16.

So, even minimally, believers are called to pray that His Kingdom be brought and implemented on Earth. Additionally, the previously mentioned verses of Isaiah 2:2 and Micah 4:1 both state that the mountain (read: God's government) of the Lord's temple would be established as the highest of all of the mountains **in the last days** and that it would be exalted in all of the hills (read: man's governmental and organizational structures) and all nations would be drawn to it. In the last days refers to the time immediately preceding Jesus' return to Earth.

Therefore, Daniel is describing the faithful followers and doers of the word of Jesus when he explained the concept of a rock, which grew to become a mountain and overtook the hills of the world (Daniel 22:45). Daniel is describing an End Times move of God through the faithful disciples and servants of Christ, which will expand and grow to encompass the entire Earth and swallow all of the established human structures and organizations, including the political structures established by men. And this concept is supported through many other Biblical texts, one of which is the much cited verse of Isaiah 11:9, "...*They shall not hurt nor destroy in all My Holy Mountain: for the Earth shall be full of the knowledge of the Lord, as the waters cover the sea.*"

The Ekklesia Takes its Rightful Place

At this point, with all that we see happening in the world, it would be an easy thing to begin to despair. There is so much darkness covering the Earth at the moment that finding a glimmer of hope in all of that is like trying to find a needle in the proverbial haystack. And yet, it is always darkest just before the dawn. Where there is deep darkness, light has an amazing ability to dispel even the darkest of that darkness.

What you are holding in your hands is the documentation of God's Kingdom structure, revealed in detail to me and backed by numerous Biblical references. The initial revelation of portions of the structure were given to the Body of Christ in 1975, when Bill Bright, the founder of Campus Crusade; Loren Cunningham, the founder of Youth With a Mission; and Francis Schaeffer, founder of the L'Abri community in Switzerland received a divine battle plan for co-laboring with God to bring His Kingdom to Earth.

The plan was so significant and so important, that a sovereign God humbled Himself to follow the constraints of Jewish Law and Biblical mandates in order to establish the validity of the message. Within the plan was prophetic symbolism that brought an additional level of understanding to the strategy.

The Hebrew meaning of the number seven points to the fullness and fulfillment of an oath or a plan. An additional level of revelation came during a telephone conversation between Marc Chironna and Lance Wallnau on the word received by Loren Cunningham and the others. During this conversation, the seven spheres of influence became "The Seven Mountain Mandate". The number seven was included, because it is the blueprint by which The Lord will ultimately fulfill His oath to redeem everything on Earth.

The mountains within the message can be interpreted through scripture to indicate governments or governmental structures set up by God. These mountains are destined to take and have dominion over the "hills" of the Earth, which are administrative structures set up by man. Their presence within the message indicates that the mandate is, indeed, a battle plan for ushering in the dominion of the Kingdom of The Lord on Earth. The interpretation, which Daniel offered for King Nebuchadnezzar's dream in Daniel Chapter 2, highlights a rock created by the hand of God, which is destined to shatter all of the existing, man-made kingdoms on Earth and to establish the Kingdom of God on Earth. According to scripture a rock is synonymous for God, for Jesus, and for all believers who build upon the words of Jesus and integrate those principles into their lives. These believers will form the ekklesia. In scripture, ekklesia is described as a large mass of rock or a boulder (Matthew 16:18).

Biblically, the Church, or ekklesia, is a group of people called (by God – **I call**) to come out from its grouping and to go out into society. Combined with the rock references within the same text, it denotes a grouping of people who base their lives and their actions upon the teachings of Jesus and the Holy Scripture called out from their place of grouping and called to move into the world affecting it with the principles and values upon which they have based their lives and their actions. This forms the basis of the Seven Mountain Mandate. The Body of Christ is being called to find, recognize and move into the place of authority that they were created to inhabit.

When Jesus taught His disciples to pray in Matthew 6:10, He admonished them to pray to God that *"your Kingdom come...on Earth as it is in Heaven"*. Jesus also taught them, in that verse, **how** God's Kingdom was to manifest on Earth: *"your Will be done on Earth as it is in Heaven"*. The Kingdom will come, when the Church begins to corporately submit to the Will of God in every area of their lives. The key to achieving this submission and to starting along a path of individual fulfillment of the Seven Mountain Mandate is to have a personal relationship to God through the receiving of Jesus Christ as your Lord and Savior. Learning how to hear God is the next step. This will require some effort on the part of a believer and might require the assistance of others.

Sometimes old wounds, hurts and life experiences leave scars on a person's psyche, soul and body. These scars can cause a disconnection between the believer and God and will more often than not make it harder for a believer to hear the promptings of The Holy Spirit. Receiving prayer, deliverance and inner healing ministration will remove those blockages. Additional ministrations for physical healing will bring the body back into alignment with the will of God. A lot of times, family histories or traditions will cause people to embark down a career path that they might not really be called to. Finding one's true calling in life is imperative to being able to fit into that spot within the Kingdom that you were created to occupy and succeed in. *The Passport to Your Identity*™ was created to help believers to find their place in the Kingdom. Under the unction of The Holy Spirit, Rebecca Rhodes, of the Institute of Leadership Development, and I wrote a series of personal assessments. These questionnaires are designed to help new Christians as well as more mature Christians that are unsure of their calling to quickly find their rank in the Army of God, their top two spheres of influence or mountains, the level of development of their God-given supernatural talents, the level of development in eleven life-skills imperative to being able to effectively take territory in their spheres of influence, and their preferred method of communication.

Since then we have been able to administer them to hundreds of people. The level of accuracy is astounding. And people have stated how the results had resonated deeply within them. In many cases, the outcomes forced them to accept truths that they had been suppressing for many years. One lady was so impacted that she quit her job, packed her bags and moved across the country to start a new career. In an email that she sent, she thanked us profusely for helping her to find and step into the job that she had always felt called to, but never had had the courage to do. Discovering and stepping into her calling was a pivotal moment in her life. It changed everything and has afforded her a quality of life that she had never dreamed of. She has the peace of knowing that she is exactly where God wants her to be, doing what God has created and called her to do. She is impacting her environment in ways and in a measure that she would never have been able to accomplish, had she stayed in the position that she was in, when The Lord confronted her with *The Passport to Your Identity*™.

I firmly believe that a motivated and educated Body of Christ will rise up and begin occupying, taking dominion, and advancing in those mountains and spheres of influence that it has been called to impact. When we begin to do that, the Kingdom of Heaven will be brought to Earth.